Best Wishes
Always

Ann Ridings
1-31-18

Thoughts Into Words

A book of Poems and Song Lyrics
by Ann Ridings

Copyright © 2017 by Sarah Ann Ridings

All rights reserved.

This book or any portion thereof may not be reproduced or used in any manner whatsoever without the express written permission of the author except for the use of brief quotations in a book review.

Printed in the United States of America

First Printing, 2017

ISBN 978-1-5323-3707-9

Blakhart Media
218 Spring Street
Huntingdon, TN 38344

Ann@MyThoughtsIntoWords.com

www.MyThoughtsIntoWords.com

The Musings and Scribblings of Ann Ridings

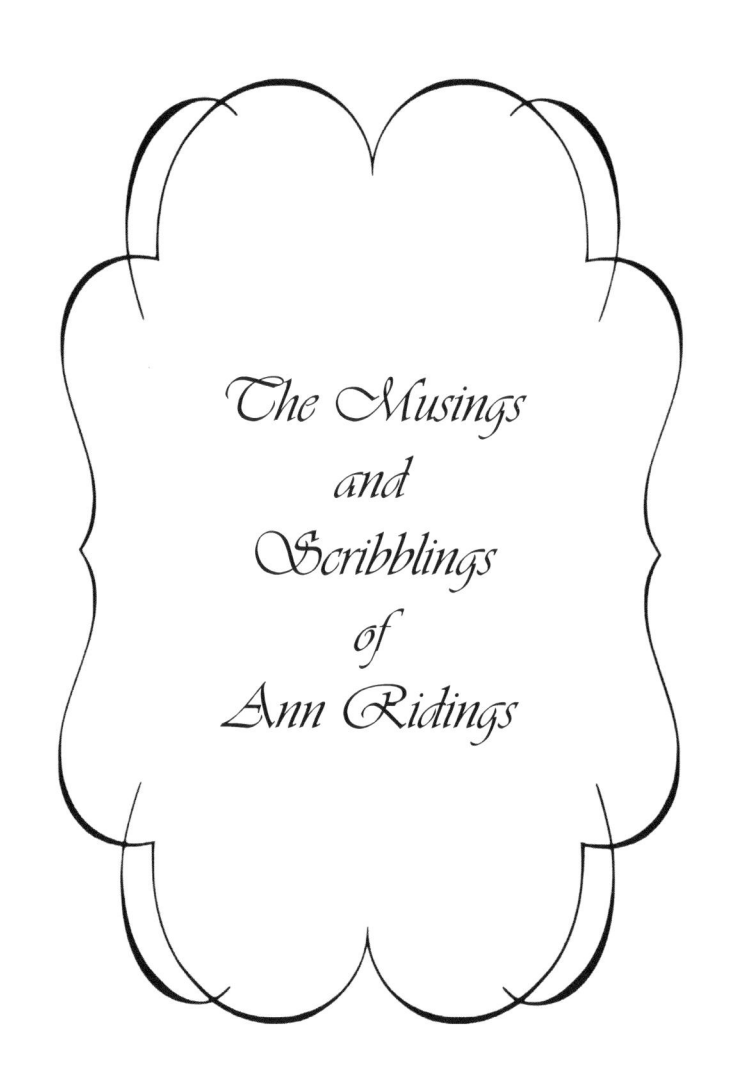

Dedication

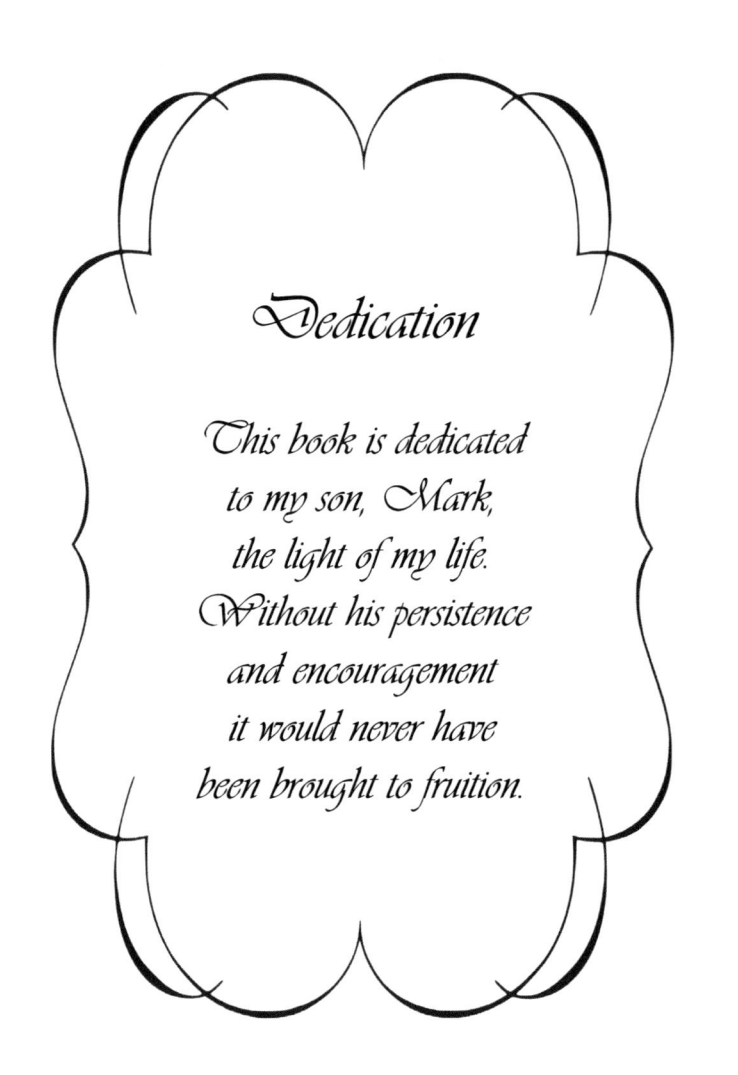

This book is dedicated
to my son, Mark,
the light of my life.
Without his persistence
and encouragement
it would never have
been brought to fruition.

Introduction

Through the years I have jotted down some thoughts in poems, songs, and such just for my own amusement, or the amusement of friends, or to express some thought I was having at the time. Some I have shared and some I have not, mainly because I thought no one but myself would be interested in reading my rambling. They were scattered here, there, and everywhere, either in a computer file (under who knows what name) or on a scrap of paper thrown in an old file folder.

For years my son, Mark, has encouraged me to get all my "stuff" together and publish a book so that he or other members of our family could read them. He persisted and finally I acquiesced . So, if you happen to be reading this book, I hope you find something that pleases you, or just makes you think, or makes you laugh. At least you will probably get an insight into how my mind works. If no one ever reads it and it gathers dust on some obscure shelf somewhere, or in a box of "stuff you don't know what to do with", that's okay. Maybe Mark will be pleased that I finally "got-er-done".

Sometimes it is hard to express just how you feel about a circumstance or situation, but I found that if I spend some quite time in meditation and let peace fill my mind and heart, thoughts do come. Then, thoughts into words.

Most of the things I have written are touched by my faith in and love for my Lord, Jesus Christ. I only regret that I am not articulate enough to express my sincere thanks for His grace and mercy. But, how can anyone adequately magnify our God? He knows my deepest thoughts, and, thereby, knows my love for Him, but it would be wonderful to have the words to express it to another human being.

If I could only touch a life and lead that life to Him, I would feel I had been of some service. I can only say, "Dear Father, thank you for the exalted privilege of being Born Again through the sacrifice of your dear son, my Lord, Jesus Christ."

Contents

Prayers and Poems 1

For Mark 37

In Memoriam 49

Nuggets from Nature 57

A Little Bit of This &
A Little Bit of That 75

An Old Fashioned Love Story 97

Song Lyrics *109*

Prayers
&
Poems

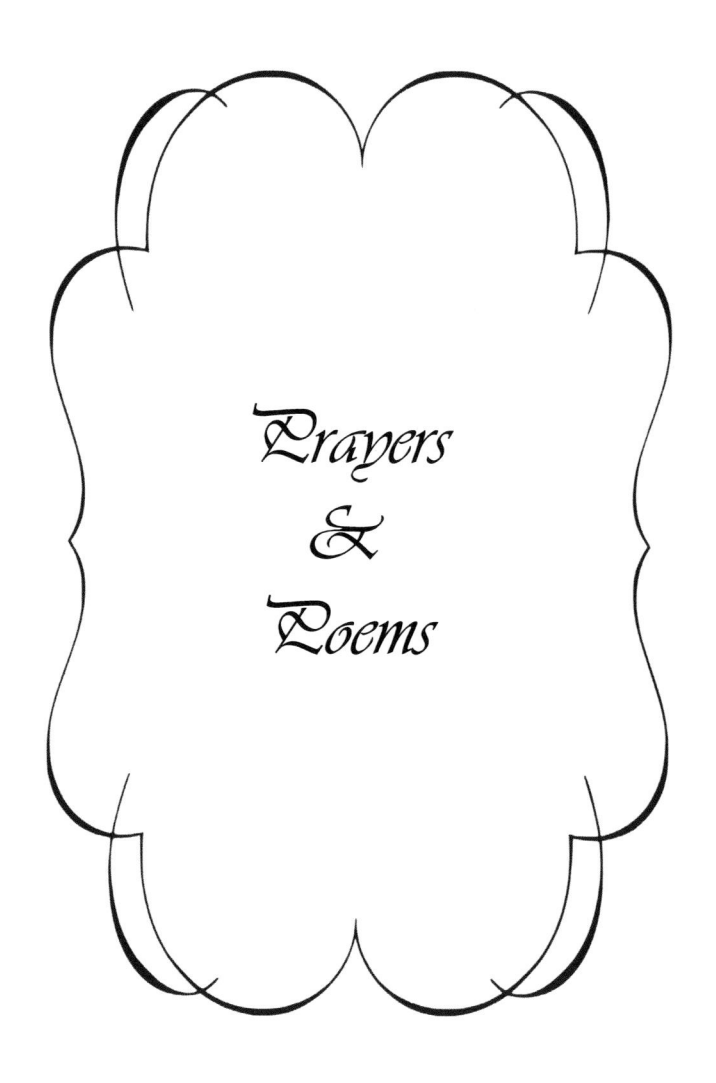

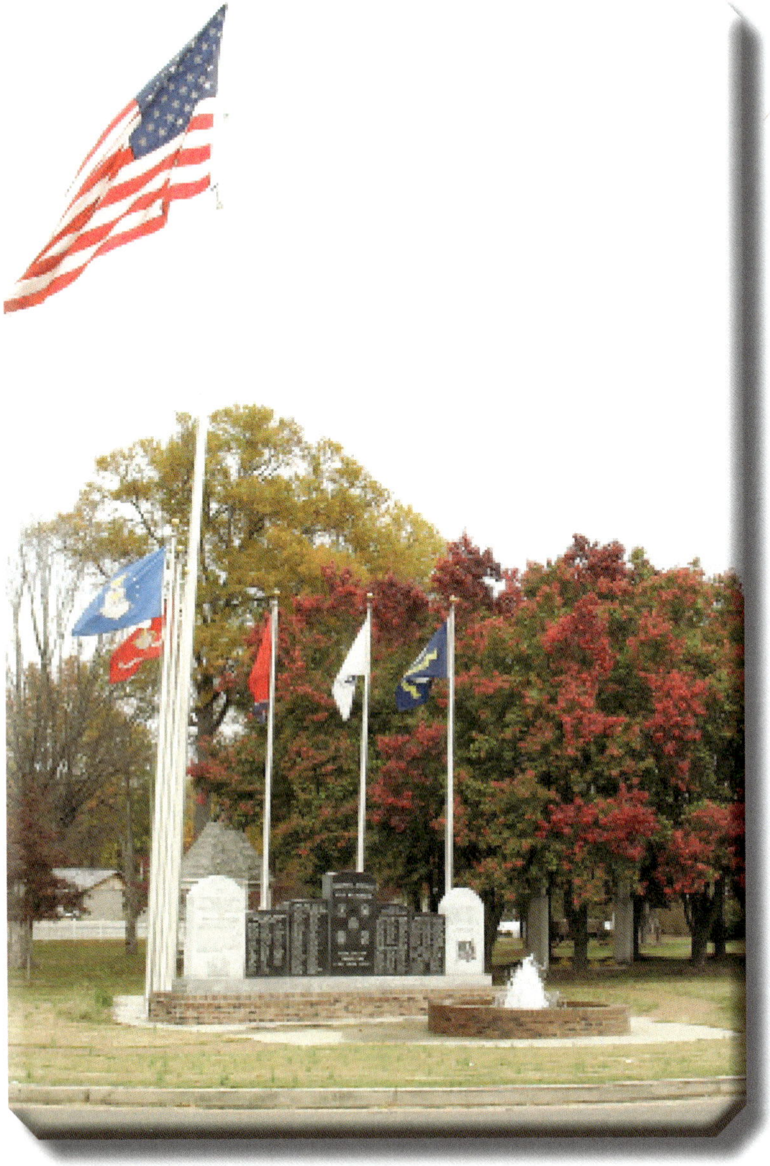

A Prayer for Memorial Day

The heritage of our fathers, past,
Has brought us to this place at last
To honor those whose faith lives on
In our churches and in our homes.
As we reflect on these things today,
Let us give pause for a moment to pray.

Our Father in heaven, may we always be
Dedicated to serving and following thee.
May your love and grace extend
To each of us, as friend to friend.
May your watchful care always endure,
May you always keep us safe and secure,
And may the faith we now confess,
Cause future generations to call us blessed.

Amen

Psalm 91:11-12
For He shall give His angels charge over thee, to keep thee in all thy ways. They shall bear thee up in their hands, lest thou dash thy food against a stone.

My Prayer

When all the world Had turned its back and gone,
And I was left to face my problems all alone,
I hid my face, and then upon my knees,
I wondered if my God would hear my pleas.
For I had strayed and was not worthy of His care,
Yet still, I hoped He would my burdens share.

Reluctantly and ashamed, I began to pray.
My heart was heavy, my words were hard to say.
"I beg, O Lord, that you would hear my plea,
I've no one else to help me, only Thee.
I know I've sinned and this I cannot alter,
But with your help, in the future, I'll not falter.

With your forgiveness, and your hand to guide me,
I'll face my life ahead with you beside me.
Forgive me for the evil things I've done.
Give me grace to face my enemies one by one.
Please hear my prayer, I beg you once again,
Erase my heart of all the sin within."

As I finished, I could not raise my head.
My burdens were too heavy, my thoughts like lead.
But, then, a soft sweet voice did all my burdens lift,
And I knew God's forgiveness
As a precious gift.

Have You Said A Prayer Today?

Have you said a prayer today,
To help you on your way,
Or thanked the Lord for blessings,
Far more than you can say?

Have you confessed your faults to Him
And partaken of His grace?
Have you stopped to think what He will say
When you see Him face to face?

Just stop and look around you
At the gifts you are not due.
What if your loving Father,
Did not have time for you?

Talk to Him today, my friend,
And open up your heart,
In every thing you do, my friend,
Make Him a vital part.

Psalm 145:18
The Lord is nigh unto all them that call upon Him, to all that call upon Him in truth.

Remember to Pray

Looking forward,
As we often do,
To things that are planned,
Some old, some new,
Our hearts fill with joy,
We can hardly wait.
We know t'will be more
Than we anticipate.

If we can get excited
About these little things,
We should rejoice even more
Over what God brings.
Blessings overflow,
Day after day.
Remember to thank Him.
Remember to pray.

I Thessalonians 5:18
In every thing give thanks: for this is the will of God in Christ Jesus concerning you.

A Prayer for Tolerance

Oh, Lord,
Help me not to criticize
The things that others do,
For I may not know the circumstances
They are going through.

It's easy to pass judgement
When things seem to be wrong,
But in Your eyes is the only place
Where truth and judgement belong.

So, keep me ever near you,
Help me keep my tongue in check.
Help me keep my eyes on you Lord,
And never turn them back.

Amen

Romans 12:16-17
Be of the same mind one toward another, Mind not high things, but condescend to men of low estate. Be not wise in your own conceits. Recompense to no man evil for evil. Provide things honest in the sight of all men. If it be possible, as much as lieth in you, live peaceably with all men.

The Bible

Someone has said that the Bible is Old,
Meant for men of another generation,
Irrelevant for today's enlightened soul,
Not really worthy of our veneration.

Such words distress me to the core,
That such thoughts could possibly be,
For I love that book even more and more
As the years pass by, for it comforts me.

To think that God in His power and glory,
Would care enough to speak to me,
Through each chapter, verse, and story,
And reveal Himself for me to see.

The Bible is God's word in a book,
And its message never changes.
It is as fresh and clear as a mountain brook,
And loftier than the mountain ranges.

The words were inspired by the Holy Spirit
To reverent men of old,
Who sometimes gave their lives for it,
For it was treasured more than gold.

"I am the Lord, I change Not", God said,
So why would He change His word?
For, from the ways of sin to the light we are led
Through the words of the Bible we've heard.

From Genesis to Revelation
You'll always find something new,
Yet, the old story of salvation
Never changes, the whole book through.

I love that old Book, so dear to my heart,
For God speaks to me, page after page.
And it always comforts, right from the start.
I'll treasure it always, for its words never age.

How many blessings one misses
When God's word they ignore.
They don't understand that life is
Just the staging for what God has in store.

For Judgment is coming, in the Bible we're told
That we'll all stand before Him, in that city of Gold.
Will some stand before Him confident and bold
And declare to God, "I didn't know. I never was told."?

How sad, dear friend, if you fall in that number
That read not the Bible, The Truth, The Way.
Stop, consider, awake, do not slumber,
For the time is nearing when you must face that day.

Comfort

When I do see your drooping head,
Your downcast stare,
Then I do want to hold you close,
Your burdens share.
For it does truly grieve me,
Make me sad,
To see someone I love
In humor bad.
For when you love someone
As I love you,
You ache to share their troubles,
Comfort, too.
You hope that by some word,
Some loving deed,
Their darkest thoughts, their cloudy day,
Into sunshine lead.
And thus to them you prove
Your love is true,
That it will last and last
A whole life through.

Isaiah 41:10
Fear thou not; For I am with thee, be not dismayed; for I am thy God; I will strengthen thee; yea, I will help thee; yea, I will uphold thee with the right hand of my righteousness.

If I Don't Love My Neighbor

If I don't love my neighbor,
If I don't love my "kin"
If I don't love the sinner,
What an awful shape I'm in!

God is Love, we all know it,
And if I don't love Him,
God is not in me,
What an awful shape I'm in!

I've got to love all my neighbors,
Got to love all my "kin",
Got to love all the sinners,
If I want to make it in.

God help me love all my neighbors,
Work and pray every day,
Show my love for my Savior,
Watch what I do and say.

If I love everybody,
If I watch what I say,
If I really love my Savior,
I will make it home some day.

Matthew 22:37-39
Thou shalt love the Lord thy God with all thy heart, and with all thy soul, and with all thy mind. This is the first and great commandment. And the second is like unto it, Thou shalt love thy neighbor as thyself.

The Gift of Friendship

Time can change so many things,
The rise of paupers, the fall of kings.
Man is powerless to change its pace,
Though he runs and pants to finish his race.

There is a thing that time can't change,
That man can't manipulate or rearrange,
God's gift to man sent from above,
A living, breathing expression of love.

That love is shown in so many ways
That it brightens our lives, though short our days,
The love and friendship that's been shown to me,
Is as great a gift as a gift can be.

Matthew 7:12
Therefore all things whatsoever ye would that men should do to you, do ye even so to them; for this is the law and the prophets.

What Is A Friend?

[One who has a close personal relationship of mutual affection and trust with another.]

May God Himself, with blessings send
Someone that I can call my friend.
Someone to hold my calloused hand
And lift me up when I cannot stand.
Someone a cup of water give,
When I need sustenance to live.
Someone a kindly word to say
When desperation fills my day.
And I will hold fast to that dear friend
Until this mortal life shall end.

John 15:13
Greater love hath no man than this, that a man lay down his life for his friends.

A Riddle

Listen, my friend,
And I'll pose you a riddle.
Life is a circle, and as we approach the end,
We are closer to the beginning
Than we are to the middle.

Old men tell tales of boyhood days,
And their memory is as clear as a written page.
But their memory fails, to their utter dismay,
About events that occurred
Just the other day.

Perhaps life was more carefree,
Less full of strife,
Filled with mischief and fun,
And the sheer joy of life.

Then, suddenly, there comes
The realization
That years have passed away.
Day faded into day,
Full of concern and obligation,
Without noting the pleasures
That are gone with those days.

Frighteningly soon,
Approaches old age,
That unavoidable curse of all men.
When death, which seems to stalk with a rage,
Completes the circle at the point it began.

And there is the riddle.
Do you find it is true?
If you're now in the middle,
More pleasure to you!

Job 14:1-2
Man that is born of a woman is of few days, and full of trouble. He cometh forth like a flower, and is cut down; he fleeth also as a shadow, and continueth not.

People

I like people, All kinds of people I see,
Tall ones and short ones,
Thin ones and plump ones,
After all, I'm a people,
And I'm fond of me.

Some I like better than others, that's true,
Especially those with a positive view.
Negative people make me feel "down",
And it's not a real pleasure
To have them around.

But all kinds of people
Have something to share,
And at some time in life,
They need someone to care.

All in all, I like people,
Of every degree.
And, if all people liked people,
What a world this would be!!!!

I John 4:7
Beloved, let us love one another, for love is of God; and every one that loveth is born of God, and knoweth God.

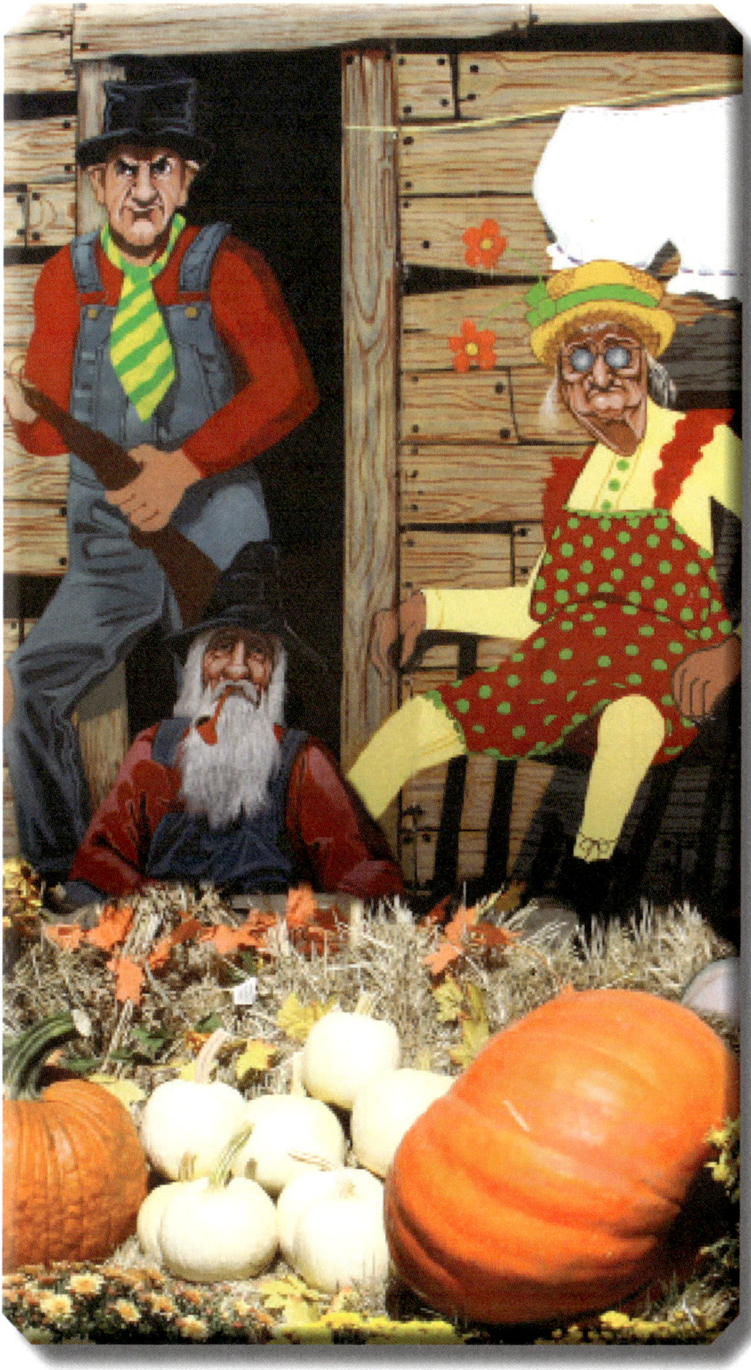

The Senses of Spring

What A Blessing --

*To feel the touch of Spring's gentle breeze;
To hear the birds in the new leaved trees;
To breathe the freshness of the world in bloom;
To know the sunshine has hidden the gloom,
To taste the goodness of God's great glories;
To see again, the oldest of stories.*

*Again, it's a paradise, as it was at the start.
Again, there are treasures to gladden the heart.
Oh! Rued is the day when it comes to an end,
And the seasons have sent us a winter again.*

Song of Solomon 2:11-12
For, lo, the winter is past, the rain is over and gone; the flowers appear on the earth; the time of the singing of birds is come, and the voice of the turtle is heard in our land.

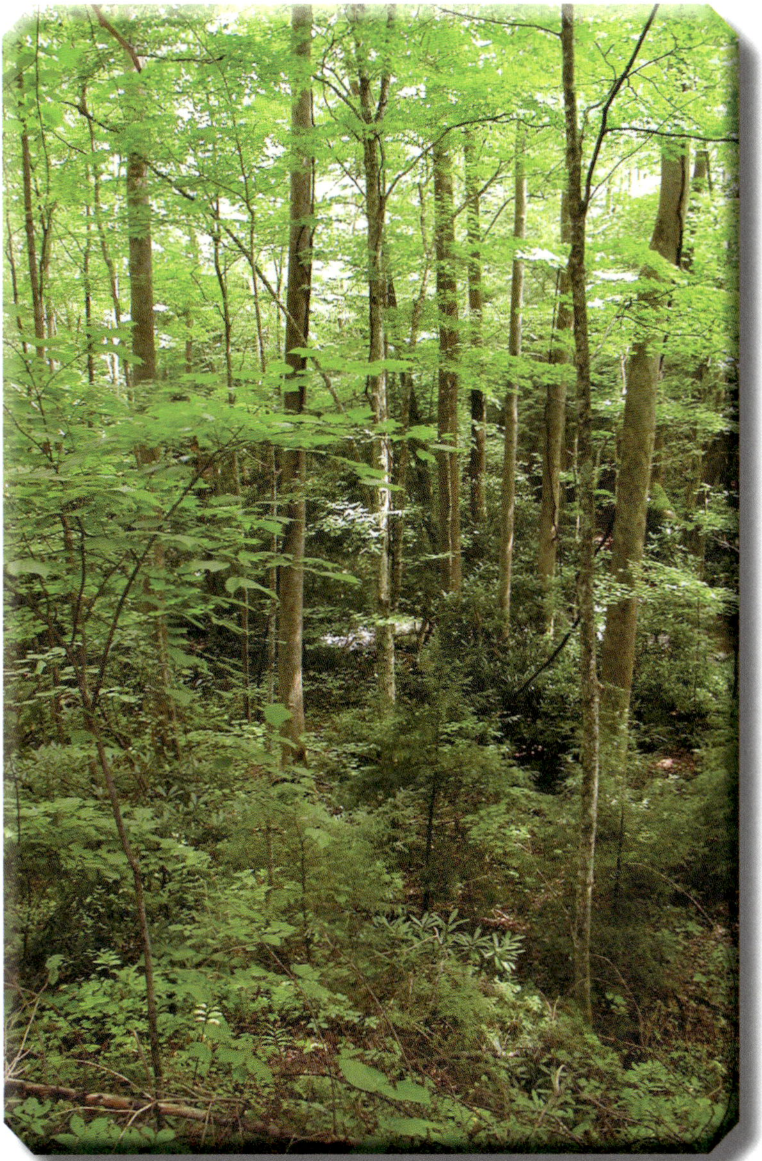

Sunrise

As the sun slips over the horizon
To light a brand new day,
My soul is filled with peace and joy,
That words are inadequate to say.

My thoughts turn inward, to another time,
When a promise was fulfilled,
"I am not dead! I am alive!
And will live forevermore."
"Believe on me and you, too, can share
This eternal life with me."

The Son arose in my heart one day,
I remember it very well.
And nothing will ever remove me from
The hands where my soul is held.

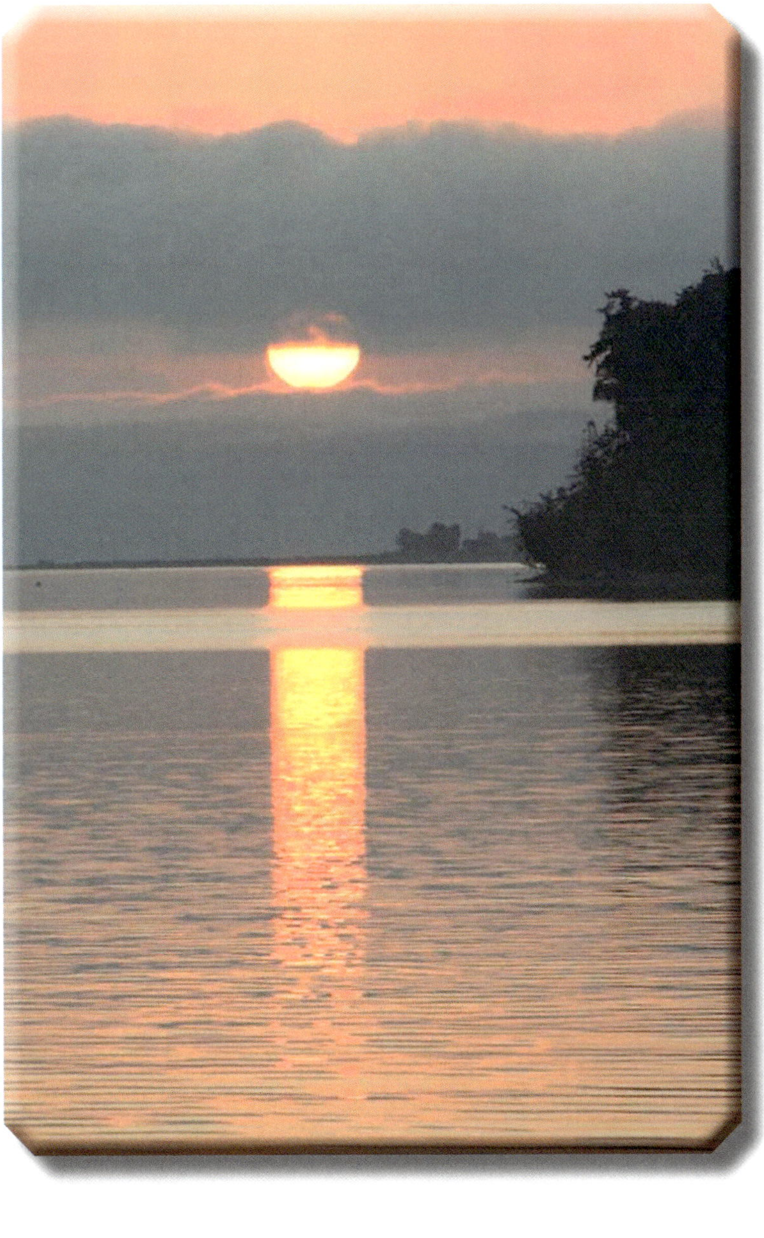

Rainbow

Mommy, how do you touch a rainbow?
"You try, my dear, you try."
Mommy, just what is a rainbow?
"It's God's painting in the sky."

Mommy, can angels touch a rainbow?
"Of course, my dear, of course."
How can they touch a rainbow?
"Because they know the source."

Do angels live with God, Ma Ma?
"Oh yes, my dear, Oh yes!"
Can they watch God paint a rainbow?
"Oh yes! They are so blessed."

Then, I would live with God Ma Ma.
"But why, my dear, but why?"
For I want to fly with angels
And paint rainbows in the sky.

[Take every opportunity to tell your child about God's wonders in the heavens, on the earth, and in our lives.]

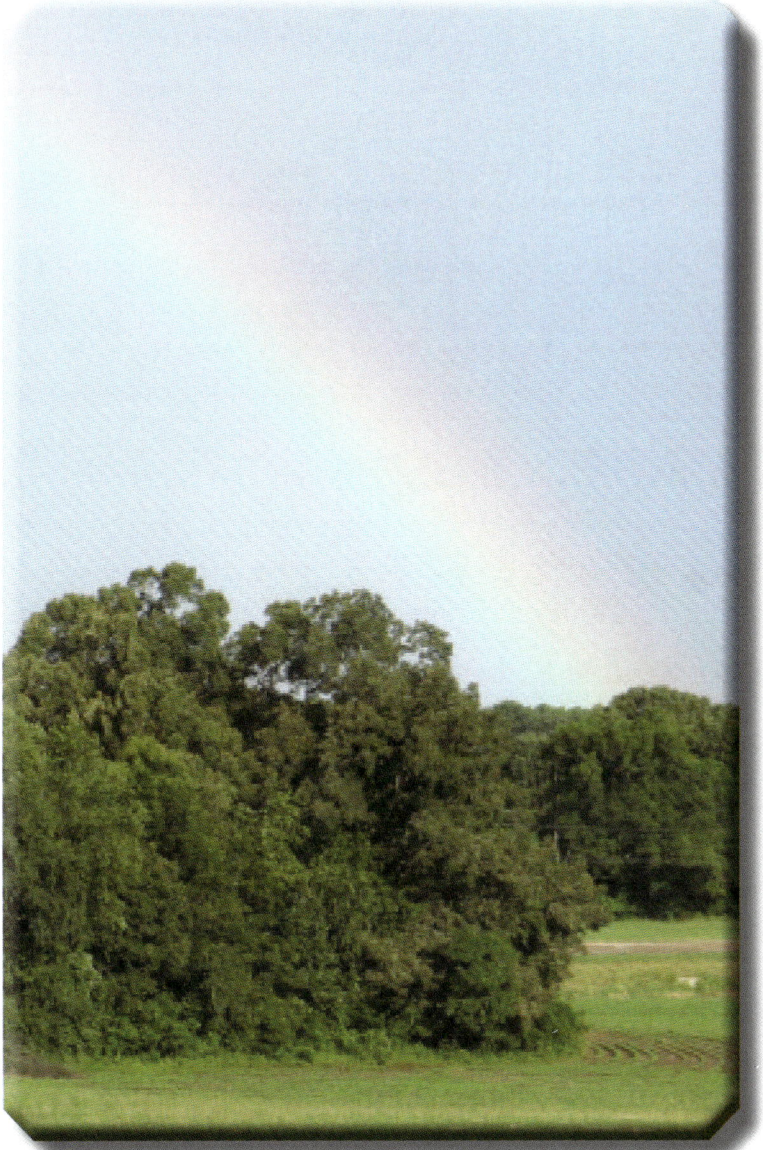

Understanding

*Some things I do not understand,
But, Dear Lord, just hold my hand.
I know you're there when e'er I call
You shall ever be my All in All.
Though dark clouds gather in these days,
I trust your will and trust your ways,
For I do know you have for me
Unspeakable bliss in eternity.*

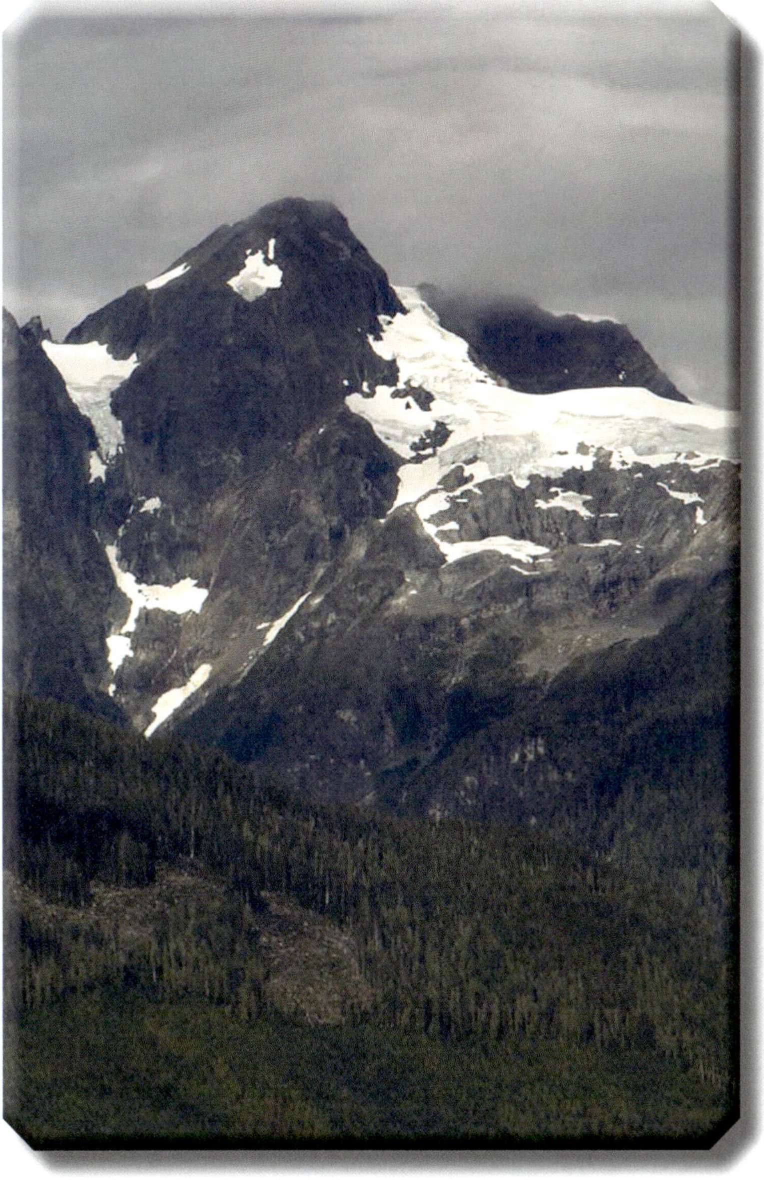

Ode to "The Age of Innocence"

(A painting by Joshua Reynolds)

Who are you little girl,
Sitting and watching the sunset's glow,
Eyes wide with wonder,
Nostrils filled with the sweet air of evening,
As the warm gentle breeze
Kisses your small red lips?

Who are you little girl,
With tender young hands
Pressed close to your breast,
Your soft brown hair
Caught up in a yellow ribbon,
With a flowing gown
Draped gracefully around you,
And there, peaking through,
Some tiny pink toes
Softly bruising the green summer grass?
Who are you little girl, so innocent, so fair?

"Who are you little girl?", I asked.
"Have you seen me and still don't know me?" she replied.
"I am you. I am you. Don't you see?
Have you hidden me so long
In your woman's breast,
That now you don't know me at all?
Look deep,
Somewhere within, I've been buried
Beneath the burdens of every day life,
Beneath your sorrow and tears.
There I still live and always will.
To find me you have only to look.
Forget for a moment the present, the past.
Open the doors of your soul.
Every woman will always have,
Hidden within her bosom
The remembrance of innocence,
And wonder, and living.
She has only to open the door of her soul
To find the girl she once was."

Who are you little girl?
Why, you're me!

The Panther

*Once upon a cold dark night,
I heard a panther yell.
And sure as I do have my sight,
It came but straight from hell.*

*I sat inside my house and listened
As it cried and cried again.
I could imagine it's eyes did glisten
And its coat was black as sin.*

*Through the swamp and through the mire,
Nightly it roams, I'm told.
They say the devil is its sire,
And thus it cries so bold.*

*I sat upon my seat and shuttered
As I remembered the stories I'd heard.
I wished I'd heard not a word they'd uttered,
Though I believed the stories absurd.*

The story goes, as I have mentioned,
That the beast does nightly roam,
But never yells without intention
Of doing harm to someone alone.

The panther's yell seemed to be nearer.
It seemed to pierce the very room.
I wished that I were not the hearer,
For the yells did speak of doom.

Then, just there, outside my window,
I saw the thing and my blood froze.
The thing, it stood, and then it bent low,
It crouched and then it rose.

It came right through the window there,
And stood upon the floor.
I could not move, but sat and stare.
I was frozen to the core.

It sat right down upon the floor,
And looked from side to side.
It looked right past me to the door.
I was puzzled and terrified.

The panther raised his head and sniffed.
"He can smell my fear", I thought.
Then he, one big black paw did   lift,
And a fluttering moth he caught.

Suddenly, he raised on all four feet,
And stretched and turned around.
He leapt right over the window seat,
Through the window onto the ground.

"What has happened?", I asked, amazed.
"Why am I not dead?"
My mind has snapped and I am crazed,
Or this is a dream instead.

As my fear subsided, I began to think
How we fear what is unknown.
And how our mind can create a link
Between what's not and what's not been shown.

In future, I will not judge a thing
By the stories that I hear,
But will seek for myself what truth can bring
From experience and knowledge, not fear.

There is a panther in all our lives
That is dark and mysterious, you see.
We have only to look and recognize
That it is there to be caged or set free.

I'll control my panther! I must, I must,
For the good of my fellow man.
For we all must build on mutual trust.
Our survival depends on that stand.

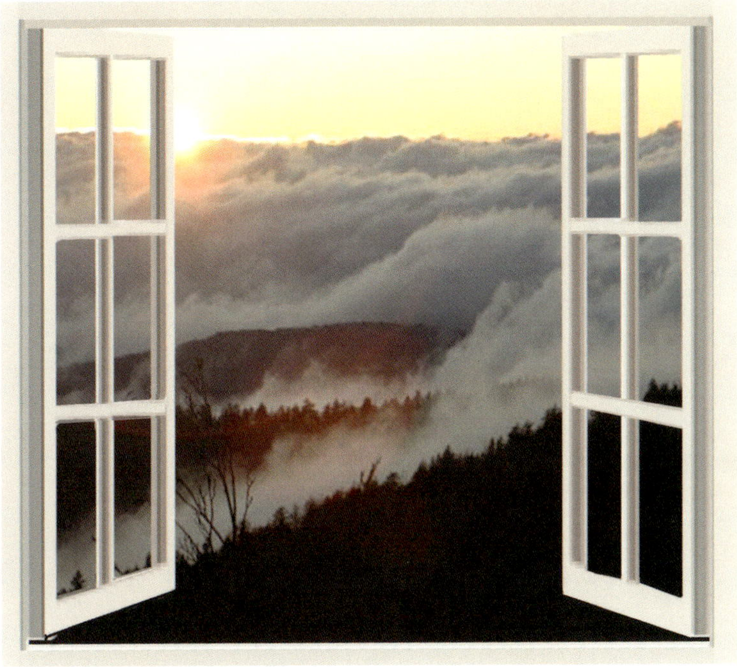

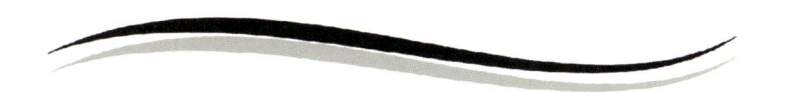

Remembering An Old Love

It's funny that throughout the years,
I can't seem to forget you.
Were you a part of some long lost dream,
That grows sweeter, as dreams often do,
Or is it just that reality,
Seems to change as years go by,
Into what we dream it could have been,
And our reality becomes a lie?

Be it reality or be it a dream,
I remember you with love;
A love without the passion
Of which youthful fancies approve,
But a love that has mellowed,
Through the years since first we met.
And a love, no less, perhaps even more,
As memories linger yet.

The passion that consumed my youth,
Ran like fire through my veins.
Your look, your touch could spark a fire,
From which ashes still remain.
Your very presence in a room,
Could heighten my senses, yet muddle my mind.
I became a trembling "nincompoop",
And no cleaver words could I find.

I found no words to tell you then
Just what I felt and thought.
I wonder if you ever knew
It was your love I sought.
I was never really sure,
That you felt the same as I,
And I could never bring myself,
To do more than wonder why.

Somehow, the years passed right on by,
You moved away, and so did I.
I've seen you briefly time and again,
And we spoke together as friend to friend,
But we only spoke in generalities,
The weather, the news, not familiarities.

Oh! How much I longed for you
To sweep me off my feet,
To tell me how you'd longed for me,
And make my life complete.
But, of course, that never happened.
I guess I knew it never would.
And, although I dreamed and fantasized,
I knew I never should.

I've lived a life apart from you,
And you apart from me.
I realized so long ago,
That we would never be.
I loved again, or thought I did,
Briefly, that is true,
But, always in my mind there was
The memory of you.

I wonder, do you think of me,
And, perhaps, what might have been,
Or have the years erased the memory,
Of a one time loving friend.
I guess I'll always think of you,
And remember for all time,
That once I loved, and felt a thrill,
That, perhaps, was only mine.

The Look

*When I perceive the
Look you cast on me,
I thank my God
That such a look can be.
So long I yearned,
And hid within my soul,
A love as warm as fire,
And pure as gold,
But would not show,
For fear of your rejection,
So trained my eyes,
To hide my heart's reflection.
Then, your look revealed
The contents of your heart,
That it was just as mine,
Right from the start.
Now when you look at me,
With eyes so tender,
My eyes reflect
My burning heart's surrender.*

For Mark

To Mark

The happiest day in all my life
Was not the day I became a wife,
But a special day, like no other,
The day you arrived and made me a mother.

Since that day, you have filled my heart
With joy and love and a special part
Of all my life will belong to you,
Now and forever, my whole life through.

I don't want to intrude upon your space,
But I do hope you will find a place
To include me anytime, anywhere,
If you ever need me, I'll be there.

From a little boy to a fine young man,
I've watched you grow, and crawl, and stand.
I've been so proud these nineteen years,
Through all the laughs and all the tears.

So on this, your special day,
I guess I would just like to say,
Thanks for all you've meant to me,
All the joy you've let me see.

May God in all His mercy give,
Happiness and joy as long as you live.
Stay close to Him and you will find
A wonderful life and peace of mind.

November 16, 1981

On Your Birthday

November 16th, 2010,
Your birthday's rolled around again,
And I remember, as I often do,
November 16th, 1962.

I was as happy as I could be
When You first looked up and smiled at me.
I remember the tiny little boy,
Who filled my heart with so much joy.

I remember fondly each year that's past.
And the memories I treasure will always last.
As long as life and time permit,
I'll hold them close and never forget.

With each and every passing year,
You continue to grow ever more dear.
Your wonderful smile, your tender touch,
Are things that will always mean so much.

I'm so proud of the man that you are now,
Your talented, smart, and know just how
To do so many wonderful things,
Can't wait to see what next year brings!

Most of all I'm proud to know
That you have faith in God - just let it grow.
If friends forsake you and life gets drear
God will comfort for He's always near.

My son, I wish I could always clear
Every stone from you path
While you're walking here,
And cause the sun to shine each day,
And bring you happiness in every way.

Always remember, I would if I could,
Because I love you and wish you good.
There's a special place within my heart
That's yours alone, together or apart.

So on this very special day,
I have a prayer that I will say,
To God who sent you here to me,
For He knows how precious a son can be.

God Bless You Forever.

Dream On My Son

Dream on, my son, of lofty things,
Of Camelot and Utopia,
For the great men of this world, my son,
Must first have had a dream.

Without a dream, man cannot achieve,
They stagnate in the pursuit of nothing.
Not knowing that without a dream,
There's no purpose in the living.

So nourish your dreams, pursue those heights,
Faint not, though men reprove you.
For those who have no dreams themselves,
Will try to disillusion you.

But, reach for the Golden Fleece, my son,
Though you know not where to find it.
It's the faithful pursuit of the goal, my son,
That makes your life worth living.

Even if the dreams you dream, my son,
May flee like the summer showers,
Remembering the pleasure of the pursuit, my son,
Will enrich your twilight hours.

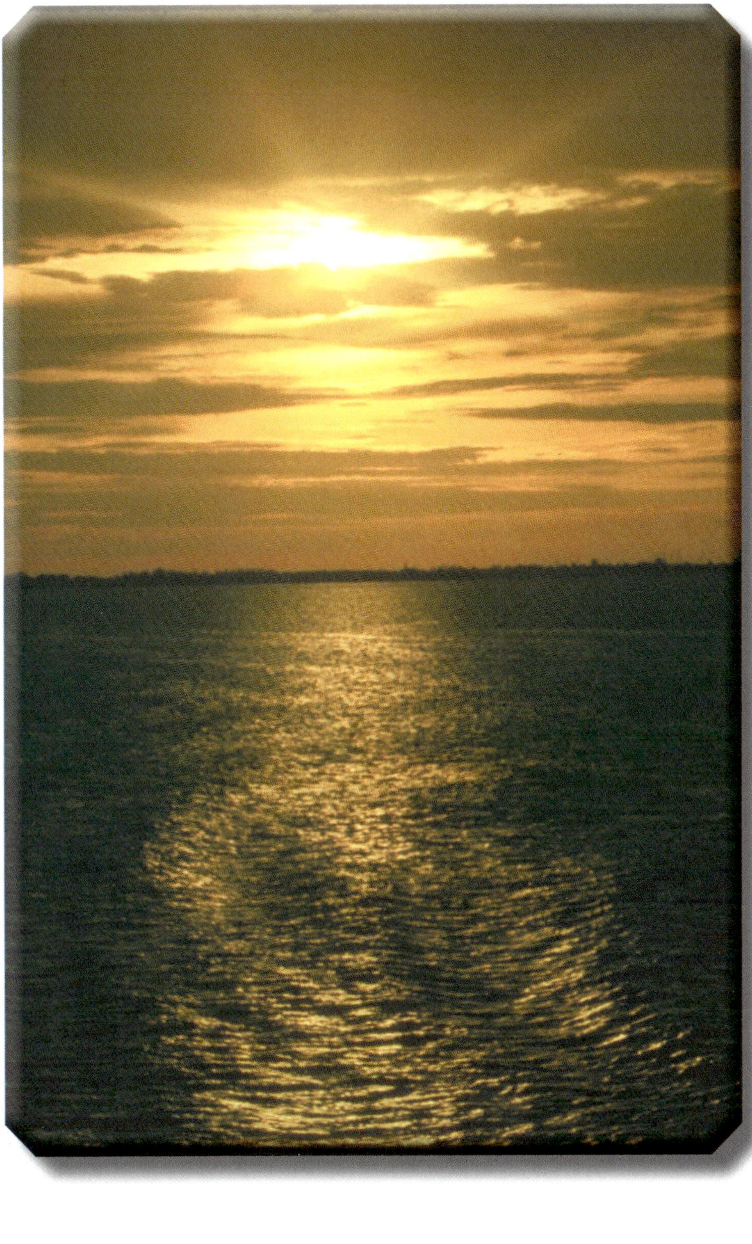

Faith

Not too many years ago
You were happy and care free,
When suddenly, tragedy struck,
Something we could not foresee.

You were almost taken from me.
The memories haunt me still.
Through days and days, unending days,
You lived by God's own will.

The pain and suffering you went through
Each hour, each day, each week
Was almost unbearable for me to see,
But my faith I had to keep!

The deepest comfort I could find
Was through God's holy word
For he opened up the scriptures
And His voice was clearly heard.

He let me know without a doubt
That He would surely heal.
We just had to trust His grace,
And His power He would reveal.

Angels He sent in the form of friends
To comfort and encourage,
To give us hope and our needs attend
When we became discouraged.

Praise God! Praise God! His blessings abound.
You are well, you are happy, you are healed!
Through it all, new strength was found,
As God's love was clearly revealed.

Your Destiny

Your destiny lies before you
Like a path through the forest green.
It turns and twists and around each curve
Is something you've never seen.

The leaves and the vines hide a multitude
Of mysterious unseen things,
Like singing birds flying limb to limb
With brilliantly colored wings.

A long tailed lizard may lie in your way,
Warming in a small patch of sunlight
Just take no notice, have nothing to say,
And he'll soon slither right out of sight.

If you follow the path before you
It may lead o'er a narrow bridge.
Be vigilant and watch your every step
For the boards may be frayed at the edge.

What wonderful sights may await you.
What experiences you may feel.
If you look only for truth and beauty,
And the things that are really real.

Expect the best to await you.
Don't bother with worry and woe.
Just look for the beauty around you,
And embrace it wherever you go.

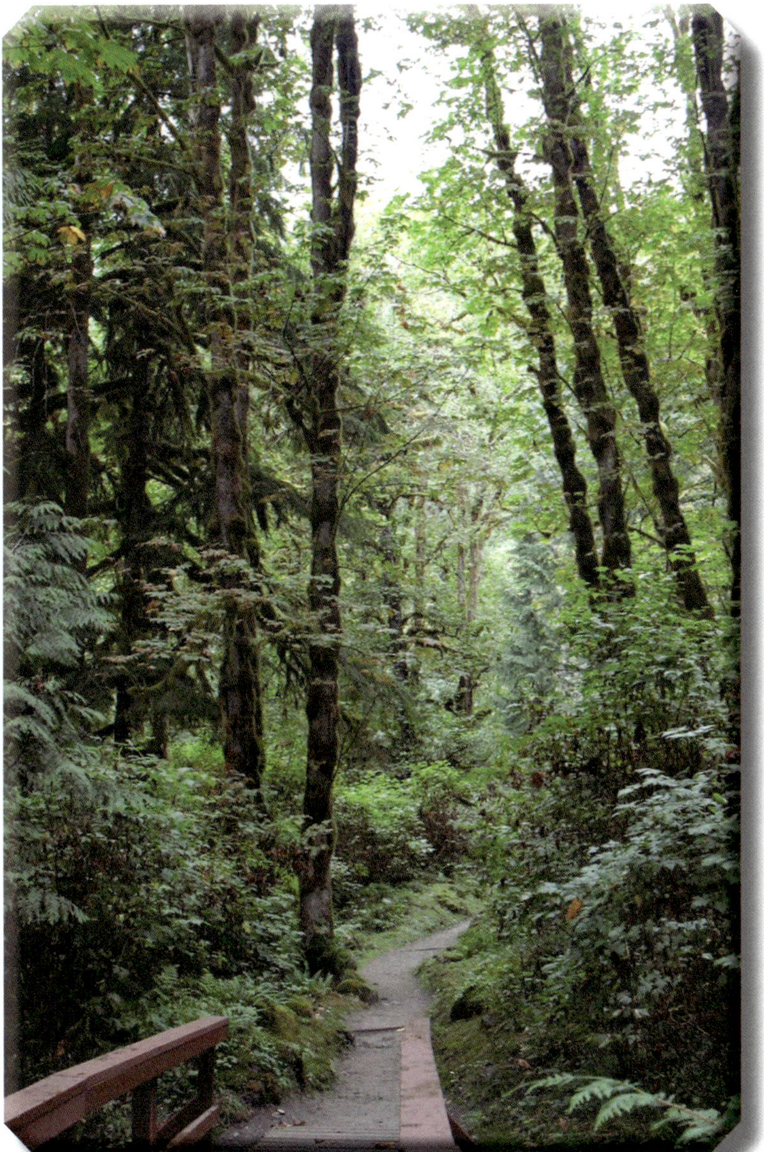

In Memoriam

In Loving Memory
Opal Robinson Kirksey Dameron
Born February 21, 1910
Died February 20, 2015

An Ode to Opal, Our Jewel

One hundred and five years ago
A jewel was born anew,
Into a family that loved it so
And nurtured it as it grew.
That jewel was taught to love our God,
And others along its way.
So, it grew and grew and it's glow became
A light to brighten each day.
As a shining example of beauty and grace,
It left it's blessings in every place.
But, now the light that it was given
Has moved itself from earth to heaven,
And there it shines even brighter still
In the love of Our Father's perfect will.

The following poem was written to be read at a memorial service for a dear friend and co-worker whose life was cut short by cancer. She was in her late thirties and she was vivacious and feisty. She walked with a bounce in her step and a smile on her face. She loved her work and performed it with vigor. She loved everyone and everyone loved her! Her first marriage was not a happy one, but she had just remarried to her High School sweetheart and her life was happy and promising until, suddenly, she was diagnosed with cancer. It attacked with a rage and she declined quickly. Then, she was gone and a great sense of loss overshadowed everyone who knew her.

Debbie, I miss you still! The memories of friends and loved ones are the treasures we cherish throughout our lives.

John 14:1-3
Let not your heart be troubled: ye believe in God, believe also in me. In my Father's house are many mansions: if it were not so, I would have told you. I go to prepare a place for you, And if I go and prepare a place for you, I will come again, and receive you unto myself; that were I am there ye may be also.

In Memory of A Friend

Life is but a breath, a sigh,
And all too soon our loved ones die.
It seems our grief we can't contain,
When our deepest heart is filled with pain.
But God above is kind and wise,
He sends our friends to sympathize.
With all my heart I send to you,
My deep regrets as we bid adieu,
To one with whom we've shared past years,
And memories that will outlast the tears.

In parting with our loved ones here,
Our heart aches, for they are so dear.
But the time will come when we shall see
Their loving face for eternity.
For as Christ himself arose from the dead,
And if by Him our hearts are led,
We shall see our loved ones by and by
In the home He's preparing in the sky.

Mary

Dearest Mary, How can you be gone?
I didn't realize you had suffered so long,
With a heart that was weary and causing you pain,
Though you didn't gripe, you didn't complain

How could I know, how could I tell,
That you were really seriously unwell?
I should have noted when your steps became slow
That you were weaker than you liked to show.

As I look back I am terribly sad,
For I know there were times when you felt really bad
And I should have been more comfort to you
And I would, if I could, looking back in review

I never thought about your heart giving way.
I guess I thought that forever you'd stay
Your own sweet self, day after day,
But God called you home and you didn't delay.

Now, I remember the good times we had,
The trips that we took, the adventures we shared,
And I want to capture and hold in my mind,
Your wonderful smile, it was one of a kind!

In Loving Memory
Mary Frances Kirksey Grissom
Born March 8, 1934
Died February 27, 2012

Nuggets from Nature

Nuggets From Nature

*Look, my eyes
and take thy fill.
These wondrous sights
are by God's will!*

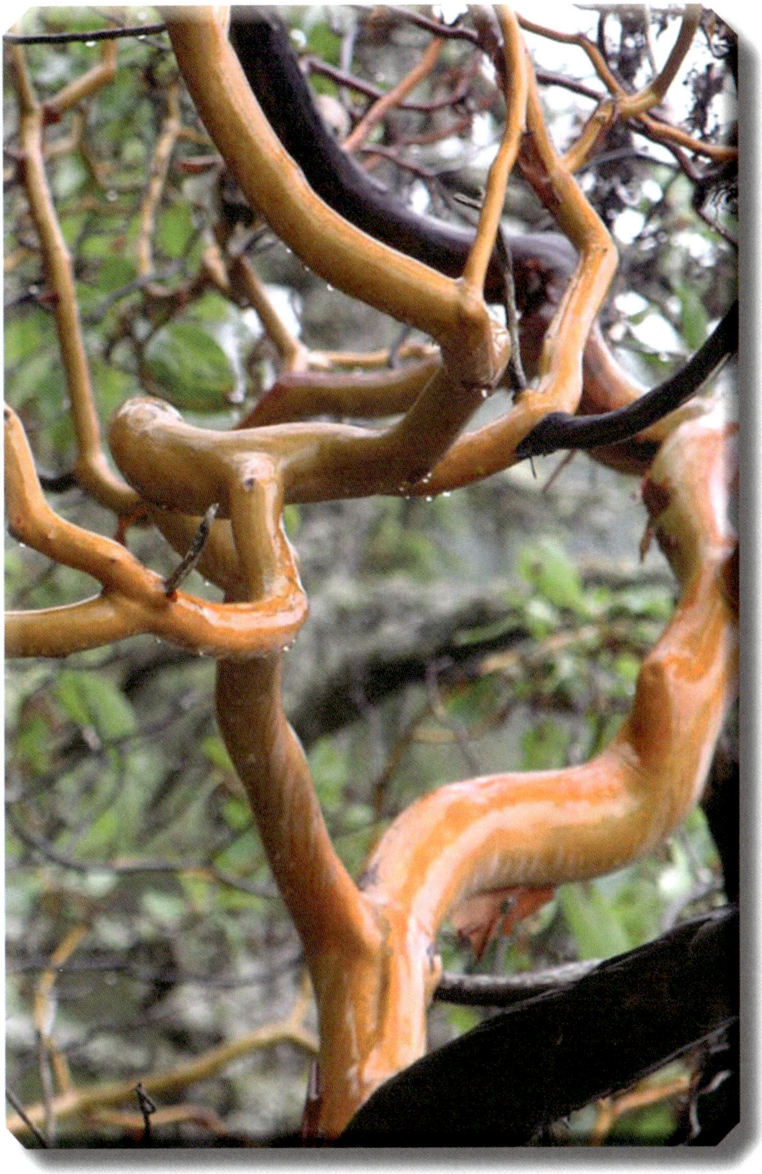

I see billowy white clouds
in a bright blue sky,
Riding on the wind
as it gently blows by,
And my heart melts within me,
a tear fills my eye,
As my soul lifts in praise,
To The
Lord God Most High

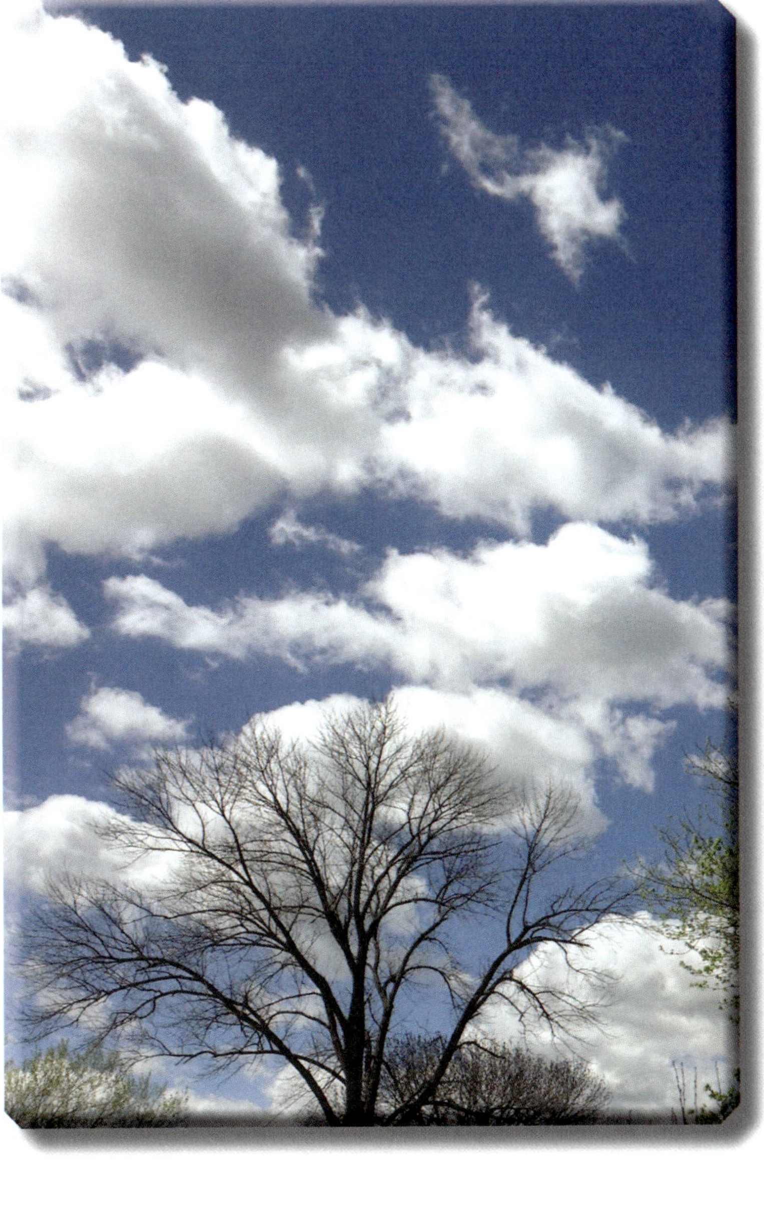

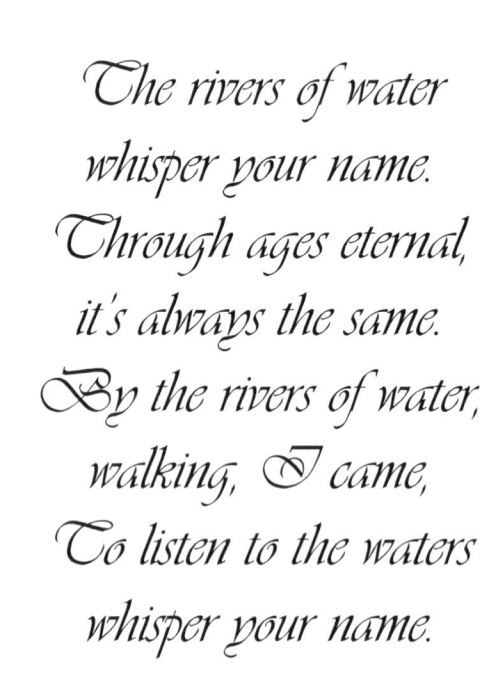

The rivers of water
whisper your name.
Through ages eternal,
it's always the same.
By the rivers of water,
walking, I came,
To listen to the waters
whisper your name.

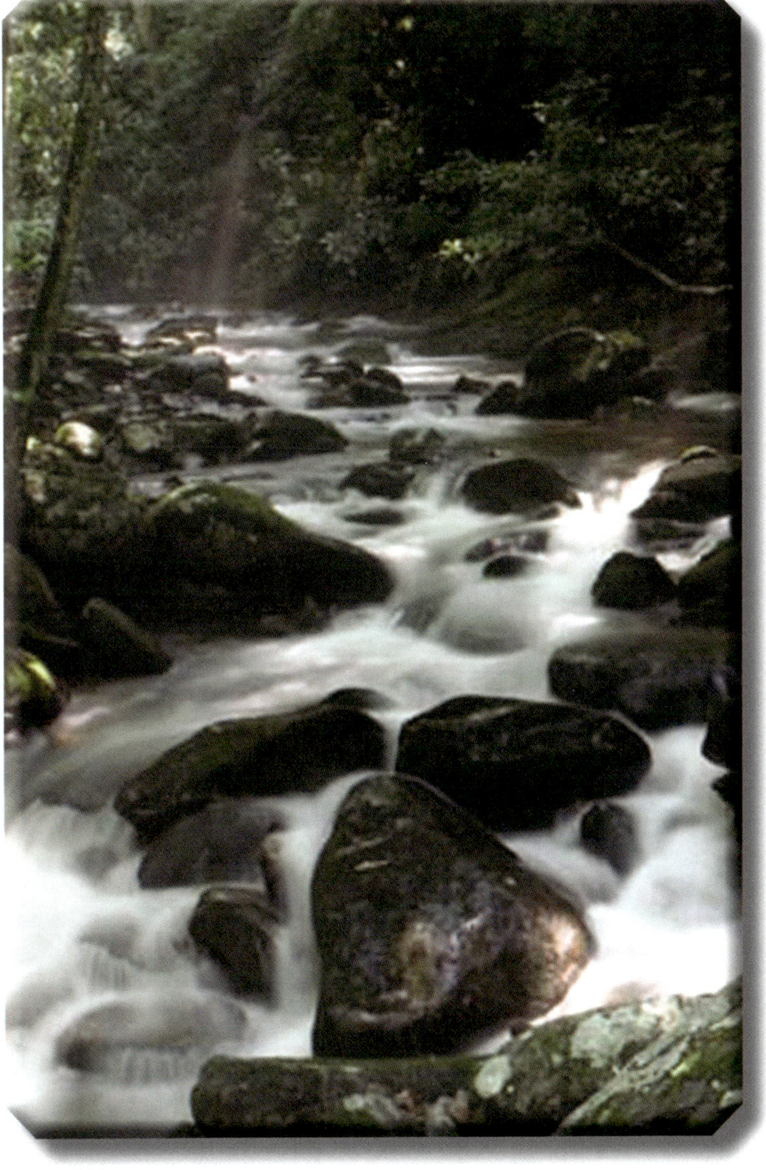

*The Autumn blaze
of nature's splendor
Shouts out, then fades,
to welcome Winter.*

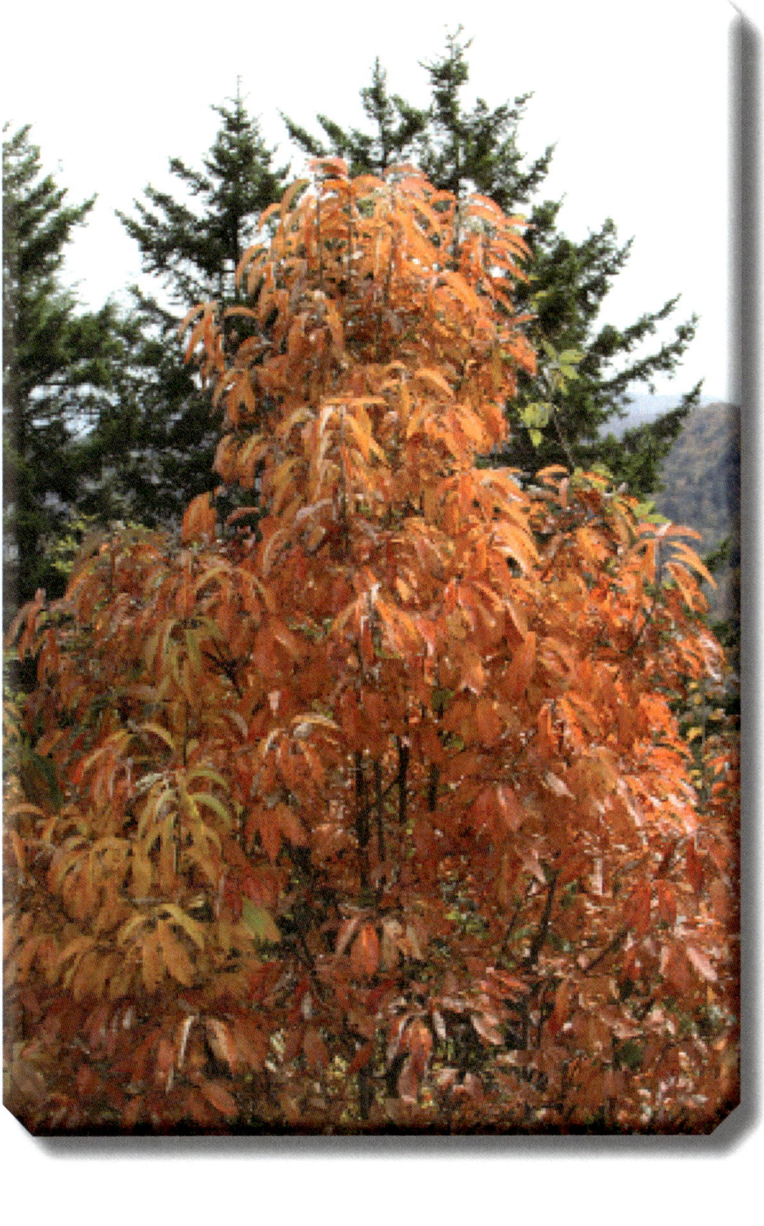

*The falling leaves
soon blanket the earth
to wait for Spring,
The time of rebirth.*

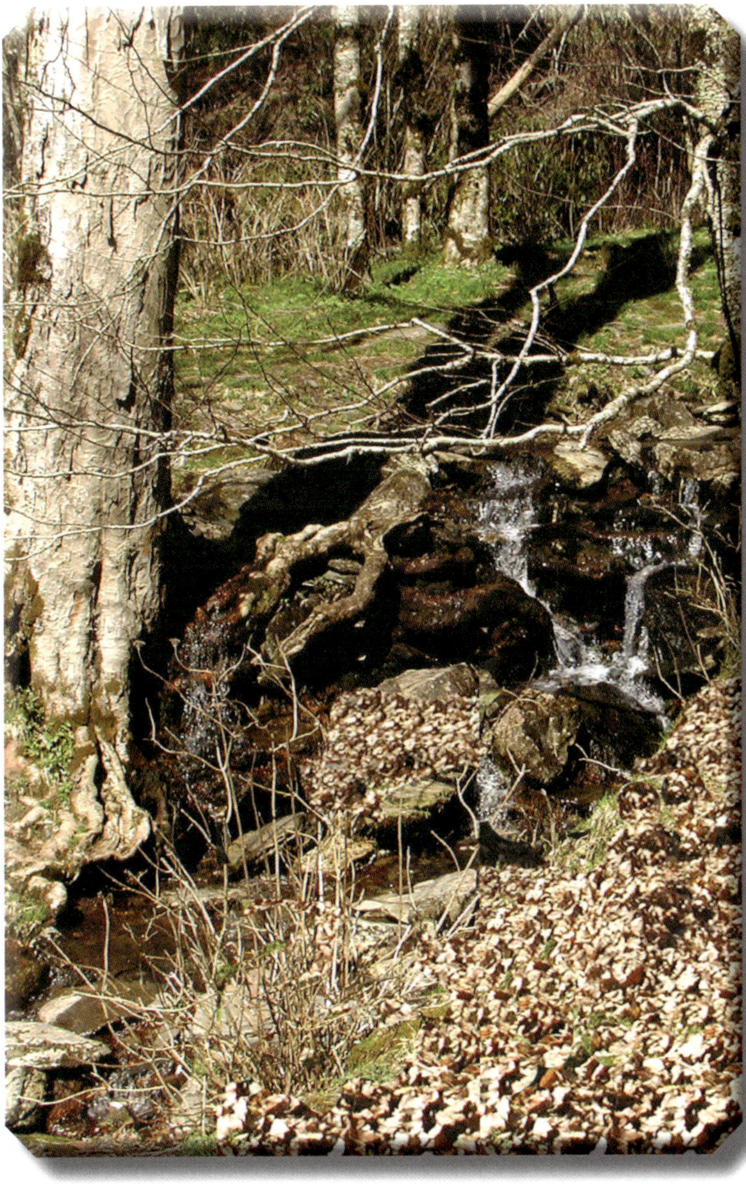

Oh, but a moment
held in time,
To inspire the artist's
soul to rhyme.
And contemplate
the reason why,
To live again,
all things must die.

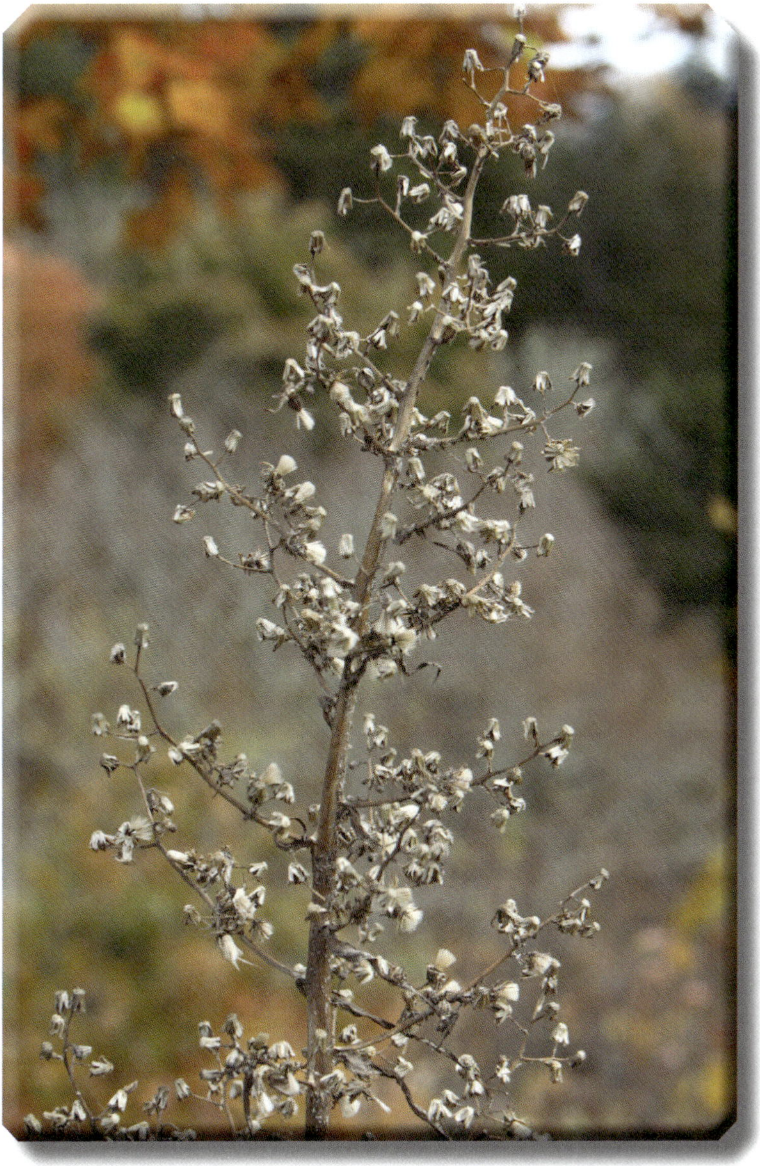

But death is life
when comes the Spring,
And all of nature
seems to sing.

For God will give
new flowers breath,
When once again
life conquers death.

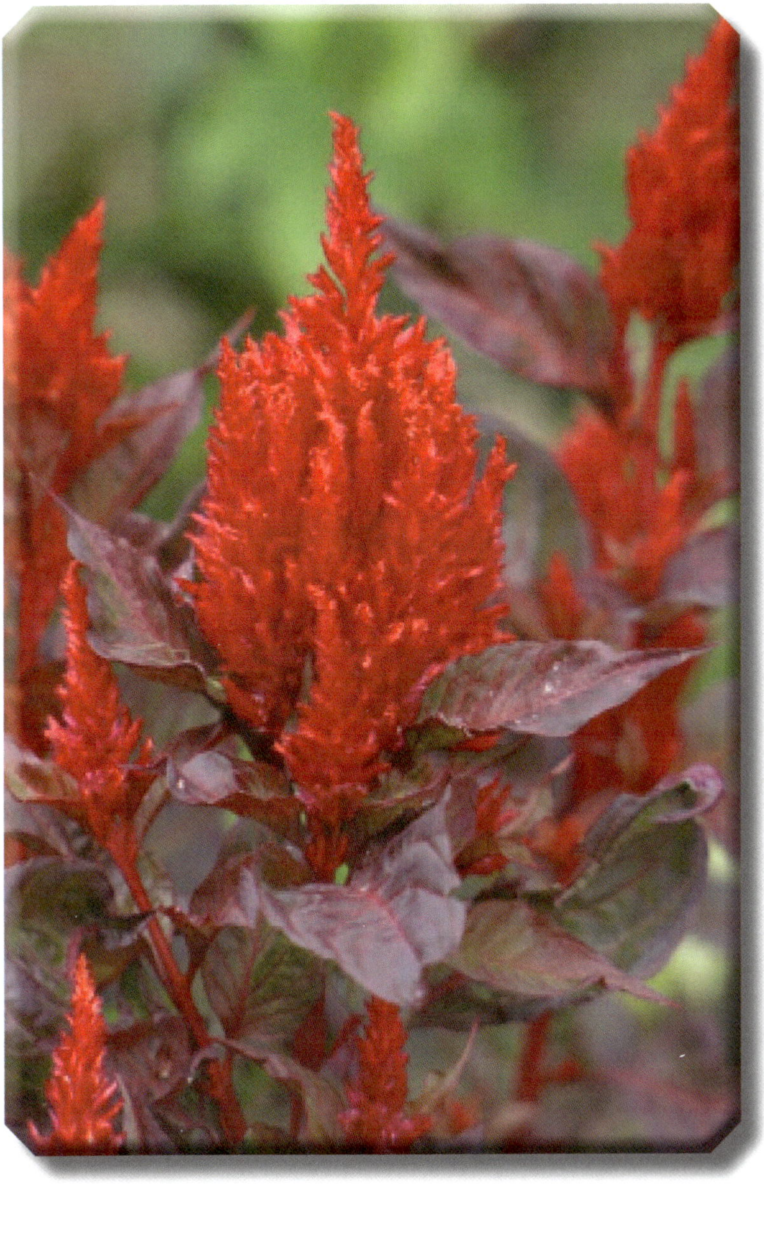

*Thank you God
for letting me see
Just how beautiful
your world can be.*

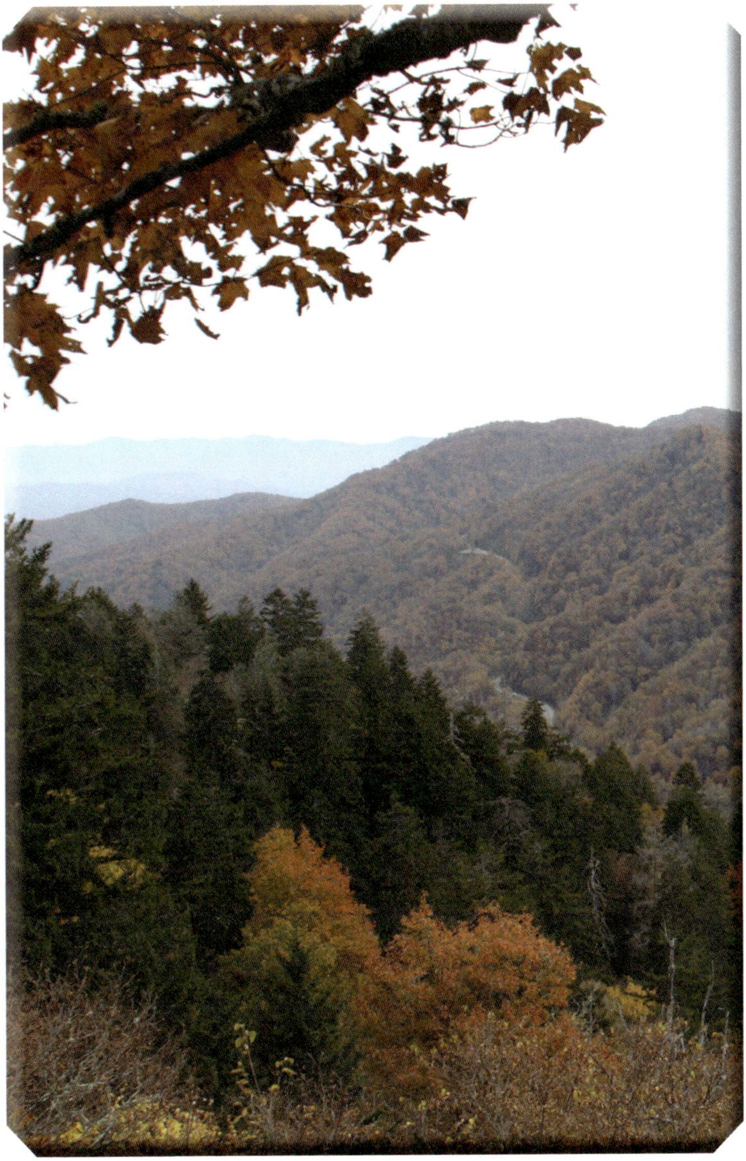

A Little Bit Of This & A Little Bit Of That

Through the years, people I have worked with, acquaintances, family, and friends, discovered that I liked to play with words and they would ask me to create a poem for a special occasion in their life. These are a few poems I wrote for those special times.

[On the retirement of a co-worker who was a source of useful and reliable information.]

The day has arrived!
I just can't believe it!
You're leaving us now!
I just can't conceive it!

What will I do?
Where will I go
For answers to questions
I just have to know?

I'll miss you, that's certain,
And others will too.
It's been such a pleasure
Working with you.

But, since you're retiring,
And we can't dissuade you
Enjoy all those interesting
Things you will do.

Take time to remember us
Now and again,
While we're still here
working
In this MESS that we're in.

Au Revoir

For A Birthday

Today is the anniversary of your birth,
The beginning of your journey here on earth.
Your days have been filled with sunrise, sunset,
With dreams that perhaps are just dreams yet.
Maybe all your hopes are unfulfilled,
And maybe some things have lacked that special thrill,
But, remember what Scarlet O'Hara would say,
My dear, "Tomorrow is another day."
As we who have passed you in years of age
Can easily tell you, as a wise old sage,
Don't let a birthday make you glum
For we know the best is yet to come!

[For a special lady who happened to be my Sister-in-law before she became my Aunt.]

For Aunt Frances

June 23, A special day,
In more than just an ordinary way.
It's special because God chose that date
A special little girl to create.
That special little girl just happened to be you,
And He gave you a book to be filled as you grew.
The pages are filled by the years that have passed
And they are unchangeable from first to last.
There are pictures and words, some happy, some sad,
But those I share with you are never bad.
The memories I have of you through the years,
Are filled with love and joy and never with tears.
I'm so thankful that you've been part of my life,
As Aunt and as Sister, when my brother's wife.
It's with great love and pleasure that I say,
Have a very, very Happy Birthday.

Written for a friend on the occasion of the 50th birthday of her twin cousins. You can guess the "gag" surprise gift she was giving them after you've read the poem.

To Velma and Thelma

Poor Velma and Thelma! They're "Over the Hill".
They've reached the age where there's seldom a thrill.
Gone are the days full of dreams and delights.
Now comes arthritis And cold Winter nights.

Life begins at forty, they say,
And for ten long years, you wait and you pray.
Then suddenly, you've reached the big five-0
And you wonder which part is the next to go.

Your friends want to help you. You can lean on their arm,
When you stumble and fall, they'll sound the alarm.
They'll say you look great, you'll feel like a winner,
And they'll furnish the teeth, when they take you to dinner.

(The gift was a set of false teeth.)

[A birthday wish for a dear co-worker.]

Happy Birthday

So, it's your birthday! Gee! That's great!
It should be celebrated throughout the state.
You deserve something special and I hope you will get
Anything you want that you don't have yet.

I can't imagine what that would be,
Cause you have so much, it's plain to see.
A spring in your step, a smile on your face.
When you walk by you light-up the place.

You have a home and family, and friends galore,
A house and a car, and so much more.
So whatever you wish, I just want to say,
I wish it for you, on your special day!.

[To My Boss on His Birthday.]

Happy Birthday

On this your very special day,
I want to take the time to say,
I think you're just the very best,
You're head and shoulders above the rest.

I never hesitate to call on you
When I'm not sure just what to do,
You always try to understand,
When problems arise, you "give a hand".

Your confidence and support I appreciate,
And, to sum it up, I'd like to state
From now until the very end,
I feel privileged to call you FRIEND.

To my Nephew when he received his "Wings" at graduation from the U.S. Air Force Academy.

Congratulations David

As you receive your Wings today,
To soar into the sky,
We pray that God will bless you,
As the days and years pass by.

May His loving arms surround you,
And keep you safe from harm.
May your life be filled with only joy,
And no cause for alarm.

May the memories made today
Be treasured through the years,
As you begin a new adventure
In your choice of careers.

The next poem was written for a friend on the occasion of the 50th Wedding Anniversary of a member of her family.

For Polk and Pearl

*Today is such a special day
For the Bilbreys, Polk and Pearl,
For fifty years ago today,
Polk wed his special girl.*

*The years, now past, have sped on by,
While day by day together,
They shared a laugh, sometimes a cry,
In sun or stormy weather.*

*This union brought in forty-three,
A bouncing baby, Gerald,
Then in forty-five, to the family tree,
Did the birth of Margaret herald.*

*Lisa arrived in sixty one
And made the family five,
The years passed on, they seemed to run,
And it was good to be alive.*

The grandchildren then began to arrive,
Sherry first, in sixty-four
Then Cara was born in sixty-five,
And we wished for even more.

In sixty-six, we were tickled pink
When Melissa came along.
We had three little angels, we did think,
For they could do no wrong.

The years that passed were filled with joy,
And matters that were weighty,
Then we were surprised with a baby boy
Named Matthew in nineteen-eighty.

Great-grandchildren are precious and very dear,
We know and we can say,
For Adam and Patrick arrived this year,
Delighting in every way.

How nice it is to have today,
This family gathered round,
And, after fifty years, to say,
Our blessings still abound.

A few more little rhymes that have been used for miscellaneous greeting cards.

(Birthday)

*On this very happy occasion,
Let us join in the celebration
To wish you joys beyond your dreams
And success in all your happy schemes.*

*Today we send this special thought
Which cannot be sold or cannot be bought--
"May God bless your life with length
And ever increase your soul with strength."*

*Then in ending, let me say,
The traditional old cliche
For it's sincere in every way–*

Happy Birthday!!!!

(Birthday)

*We just heard a rumor ,
And we think it may be true.
We weren't really certain,
So we're checking it with you.*

*We wouldn't want to miss it,
If you're celebrating once again,
The day of your exceptional birth,
The day your life began.*

*We would want to congratulate
A dear and cherished friend,
And wish for you the blessings
Our Father God can send.
So,
God Bless You and Have A
Happy Birthday!!!!*

(Encouragement)

*May God's Mercy
And God's Grace
Be with you now,
And help erase
All the sorrow
And all the pain
And bring you
Blessed peace again.*

~~~

*May the Mercy
And Grace of God
Be with you now.
May His loving arms
Enfold you and
Bring you comfort and healing.
We want you to know that
You have friends who care
And are keeping you
In their prayers.*

~~~

*When friends are apart,
Discouraged, or sad,
Knowing you're thought of
Can make your heart glad.
So we hope when you get this
You'll know that it's true,
That someone is thinking and
Caring for you.*

~~~~

*May it comfort you to know
That you are in our hearts
And in our prayers.
The trials you are going through
Perhaps will only strengthen you
For you know you have a Friend
Who'll be near through tick or thin.
Just trust in Him for every need
For Jesus is a friend indeed —
And so are we.*

~~~~

*May it comfort you to know
That you are in our hearts
And in our prayers.
God can comfort as no one else can,
And we can take our cares to Him,
For He is always near,
And know that in His loving arms
We are safe and secure.*

(Sympathy)

Although we know we were born to die,
It brings us pain to say goodbye.
Parting, even for a while,
From those we love cannot bring a smile.
But deep within our hearts we know
Parting is only here below.
For some glad day on heaven's shore
We'll meet again to part no more.
~~~~
May the Grace of our blessed Lord
Comfort you in your hour of sorrow.
And may His abiding Love full your heart
With Peace at the thought of your loved one
In His tender care.
~~~~
In parting with our loved ones here,
Our heart aches, for they are so dear,
But the time will come when we shall see
Their loving face for eternity,
For as Christ himself rose from the dead
And if by Him our hearts are lead,
We shall see our loved ones by and by
In the home He's preparing in the sky.

(New Baby Congratulations)

Soon you'll hold a brand new life
Within your loving arms.
You'll smile with wonder and with awe,
And try to keep him safe from harm.

Believe it or not, it's a new beginning,
You'll learn and so will he.
You'll lose some sleep, there'll be rough times,
But it's worth it, wait and see.

When he looks up and smiles at you,
Your heart will melt with love.
There's nothing like a beautiful child,
Sent from God above.

So, enjoy each day, each month, each year.
They'll pass so very fast.
Before you know it, he'll be grown,
But the memories will last.

My name is Ann, of course, and a very special friend of mine happened to be writing me a nice letter expressing her high regard for me, when her sister-in-law who is also named Ann, saw the letter and mistook it for a letter to her. When she discovered it was meant for someone else, her feelings were hurt. She was disappointed, or perhaps jealous, that my friend might think more of me than she did of her. My friend was very upset, fearing she might have lost the affection of her sister-in-law, so she asked me to write a poem for her to give to her sister-in-law explaining the situation. This is that poem.

To Ann

I feel I may have hurt you,
Which is the last thing I would do,
When, quite by chance, you saw a note
To my best friend, not to you.

That dear, beloved friend of mine,
I've known for years and years,
We've shared so very many things,
Through laughter and through tears.

If you knew her, just as I,
You'd understand, I'm sure,
And any concerns you might have now,
Knowing would prove the cure.

But you, my dear, dear Ann,
Are so special and so rare,
That it would be impossible
To equate or to compare.

As wife and mother, sister and friend,
All would say you shine.
Your light and warmth enfolds us all
With love that is sublime.

So, please take comfort in what I've said.
Please put your cares to rest.
Knowing you, I can freely say,
You're better than the best.

The following poem was written especially for a Christmas program at our church. It's been used several times for that purpose.

A Christmas Poem

*It may not have been in December
Probably not the twenty-fifth,
But in Bethlehem of Judea
They story told was not a myth.*

*A baby was born in a stable,
His mother a virgin girl,
He was to speak words of eternal life
That would spread throughout the world.*

*A lowly setting for a King,
A stable not His own,
But He would rule His kingdom,
From a God given throne.*

Hallelujah! Sang the angels
As they announced His birth that night.
Shepherds watching heard them sing,
And wondered at the sight.

Wise men followed a wondrous star
That led them to the child.
There they beheld the King of Kings,
And worshiped for a while.

We know the story, Oh! So well,
We've heard it o'er and o'er
It matters not the time of year,
Let's tell it now once more.

An Old Fashioned Love Story

Daisy's True Love

Daisy's True Love

I

Once in a glen lived a maid fair and pretty
She worked in her garden and sang her a ditty.
She sang of her lover who called on her nightly,
Who kissed her white hand and bowed most politely.
At night she would dress in a gown bright and merry
And wait by the rose covered gate for her Terry.
She would wait, she would listen to hear him approaching,
But when he arrived it would take him some coaxing,
To get the fair Daisy from acting so shy,
For she blushed and she sighed to have him close by.
He took him her hand and he bowed most politely,
And kissed her white fingers, but ever so slightly.

II

Now Daisy was fair, as I told you before,
And her age lacked but four years of being a score.
Her eyes were the color of the blue evening sky,
And her hair was as golden as the sun passing by.
Her voice was so soft and sweet and merry,
But, alas, let me tell you of her dear lover Terry.
His hair was as black as a crow, I swear it.
He was bold and was brave, anything he would dare it.
He stood over Daisy, taller by a head,
A right handsome fellow, so everyone said.
His eyes were as black as the night, so they were,
But so soft and so gentle when they looked upon her.
To see them together was a right pretty sight,
Standing and talking there in the night.

III

Too soon came the time when to home she must send him,
Or else would her Pa with a pole come and bend him.
And so, she'd give him her hand and he'd kiss it,
He'd bow most politely and say that he'd miss it,
Then off he would go on his horse, white as snowflakes,
And reach him his home as the sun a new day breaks.

IV

One day in a carriage so bright and so shiny,
Arrived a new neighbor so beautiful and tiny.
A princess she seemed, or a queen of the fairies.
Among all the eyes that she captured were Terry's.
She flirted and flounced in her gowns so expensive
That her beauties were known in parts most extensive.
Her eyes fell on Terry, the poor innocent lad,
And the way that they held him was indeed truly sad.
He was flattered and teased as were all of the rest,
And was made the subject of many a jest.
But Terry was blinded by the dark red hair,
And the white of her arms and the warmth of her stare.
He forgot to remember that Daisy so fair
Was standing and waiting at her gate out there.

V

Poor Daisy, she waited and waited so long,
That she could but wonder what had gone wrong.
The tears that appeared in her eyes as she waited,
Soon ran like the water of a dam that ungated.
A stranger, a passer, he noticed her there,
And he stopped and he looked and indeed, could but stare,
For he saw that dear Daisy was sure broken hearted.
He hated to leave her and go on as he'd started.
He stopped and he wondered just what he should do,
Because he'd not met her, to her he was new.

VI

The stranger was as tall as Terry, I'd say,
But looked as if the price of a meal could not pay.
His eyes were as gray as the morning's sky bright,
And his hair was the color of a moonless dark night.
His heart was as pure as a lamb, I am sure,
But he was wise in the ways of the world and it's lure.
When first he did look upon the fair weeper,
He knew o'er his heart she would always be keeper.
For never in all of his travels had he
Seen one he could love, but here, only she.

VII

He walked up to her and he asked her the matter.
She looked up and saw that his clothes were a tatter,
But she looked to his eyes and in them were shining
A love and she knew that for her he was pining.

They sat down and talked and she told him the matter.
She told him her heart was at present a'shatter.
She told him her lover had proven untrue,
 And now he was claiming a lover new.

VIII

The new found friend was gentle and kind,
He helped her there to ease her mind.
She asked him if he would visit again,
He said that he would, could he find an inn,
To rest his feet from the long, long journey,
And look for a job to earn him some money.
So Daisy, she told him of an inn in the town
Where he could rest his tired feet and sleep, oh, so sound.
So he left her then and he went him his way,
And he promised he'd come back the very next day.

IX

He found him a job on a farm near at hand,
Plowing the fields and working the land.
Each night as the sun was sinking low,
To Daisy's he'd off and away he would go.
Now Daisy's Pa was a right good man,
And he liked this young lad with the strong firm hand.
They sat and they talked 'til late in the night,
The friend, he talked of his travels, his strife,
And the old man talked of his own past life.
Daisy, she learned to love this dear lad,
Whose name by now I must tell you was Chad.

His heart was so kind and so understanding,
She knew that his love would be gentle, undemanding.

X

One night when the moon was shining so brightly,
And it laid it's faint glow on the roses so lightly,
Chad took the sweet Daisy in the garden a'walking,
For he wanted to do some serious talking.
He stopped the fair Daisy and he took her small hand.
He bade her to sit and please, to not stand.
She sat, and then, down on his knee,
He knelt and he said, "I love only thee.
I hope you love me one happy day,
When thoughts of Terry have faded away."
She raised her hand and his brow she did stroke.
She opened her lips and almost spoke,
But, alas, from the house, a cry she did hear,
And Chad, he arose, it had, too, reached his ear.
They ran them together to see to their horror,
Daisy's Pa lying dead, Oh! Great was their sorrow.
So they buried her Pa the following morn,
And flowers from her garden his grave did adorn.

XI

One day Daisy was at home all alone,
When up walked poor Terry, his face like a stone
So white and so hard were the lines on his face,

That she was afraid and would have run from the place.
But he did detain her and held her so fast,
That she thought for a truth that she would not last.
He told her to listen to his sad hearted plea.
He'd made a mistake, yes, that he could see.
He loved not the girl with the long red hair,
But she, sweet Daisy, so pretty and fair.
He then let her go and she sat ere she swoon,
For she had thought this was surely her doom.
She told him as soon as she gathered her strength,
That she had waited and waited at length,
But he had not come and now was too late,
For a stranger had appeared one night at her gate.
He'd brought her a love so strong and so true,
That now she did love him. He'd not make her blue.
So did poor Terry turn around and depart,
And longed for the love he'd had at the start.

XII

Chad came to see Daisy that very same night,
And in a new dress, she was truly a sight.
So pretty was she that it fare took his breath,
(It was now past a month since her dear Pa's death.)
Each night he had called in the usual way,
Yet never another love word did say.
They walked to her garden and there took a seat.
Daisy opened her mouth and to Chad she did speak.
"I love you, my dearest, I know now it's true,

For I have seen Terry, but my thoughts are of you."
He took her and held her so close to him there,
They both were so happy, they had not a care.

And so ends this tale of love's joy and sorrow,
Just as life is lived from one day to the morrow.

Song Lyrics

Humbleness

A worm am I.

A grain of sand upon the shore,
Nothing more.

A speck of light in a star filled night,
Out of sight.

A worm am I.

Scripture

David said in Psalm 22:6
    But I am a worm, and no man; a reproach of men, and despised of the people.

John 3:16
    For God so loved the world that He gave His only begotten Son that whosoever believeth in Him should not perish, but have everlasting life.

Why Does He Love Me?

When the trials and toils of a long busy day,
Leave me tired and weary, and filled with dismay,
My comfort and solace comes from above,
Sent by a Savior and given with love.

Chorus:
Oh! Why does He love me?
Oh! Why does He care?
I'm so unworthy, sometimes I despair,
Then He in His kindness, looks down from above,
Lifts up my soul, and fills me with love.

God in His mercy, sent down His sweet Son,
The crown prince of glory, to save everyone.
He lived as a man, He bled and He died,
He arose and returned to His place at God's side.
(Repeat Chorus)

He's there when I need Him, I know that He cares.
Every need He supplies, every burden He bears.
When my trials and toils on earth are no more,
He'll be there to welcome me through Heaven's door.
(Repeat Chorus)

Scripture

Matthew 11:28-30
Come unto me, all who labor and are heavy laden, and I will give you rest. Take my yoke upon you, and learn from me, for I am gentle and lowly in heart, and you will find rest for your souls. For my yoke is easy, and my burden is light.

John 14:27
Peace I leave with you; my peace I give to you. Not as the world gives do I give to you. Let not your hearts be troubled, neither let them be afraid.

John 16:33
I have said these things to you, that in me you may have peace. In the world you will have tribulation, but take heart; I have overcome the world.

I've Found A Peace

I've found a peace the world cannot supply,
I found it in the Lord of earth and sky.
A peace that only faith can make secure,
And a faith that only God can make endure.

Chorus:
I thank Thee, Lord, for each new day,
The sun that shines along my way,
When trials here shall be no more,
To heaven's gates my soul shall soar.

I am just a sinner in His sight.
Only faith in Christ can make things right.
I try to find a time to steal away and pray
That the Lord will help me make it through each day.

I thank the, Lord, for saving my poor soul.
I thank him for each blessing new and old.
I know without His hand to guide me, I would fall.
So I thank Him every day for it all.
(Repeat Chorus)

Help me conquer each temptation thrown my way,
That I may help some soul whose gone astray.
Lord, make of me a tool within thine hands
That I may be a special blessing in this land.

When time shall come for me to bid farewell,
To things I've known and those I've loved so well,
On angels wings my soul shall fly away,
And I will live with God in that eternal day
(Repeat Chorus)

Scripture

Genesis - Chapter 1:1 - 31   (Abbreviated)

V. 1 - In the beginning God created the heaven and the earth.

V. 2 – And God said, Let there be light and there was light ----and the evening and the morning were the first day.

V. 6 - And God said, Let there be a firmament in the midst of the waters, and let it divide the waters from the waters. And the evening and the morning were the second day.

V. 7 - And God said, Let the waters under the heaven be gathered together unto one place and let the dry land appear, and it was so. God called the dry land Earth.

V. - 12 And the earth brought forth seed yielding vegetation at God's command and the evening and the morning were the third day.

V. - 14 And God said let there be lights in the heavens. He made two great lights, the greater one to rule the day and the lesser one to rule the night. He made the stars also. And the evening and the morning were the fourth day.

V. - 20 And God said– let the waters bring forth living creatures and foul to fly above the earth in the open firmament. And all the living creatures were made to bring forth after their kind. God blessed them and said be fruitful and multiply. And the evening and the morning were the fifth day.

V. - 24   And God said, Let the earth bring forth living creatures after his kind, cattle and beasts and creeping things

V. - 26 And God said, Let us make man in our image, after our likeness–So, God created man and gave him dominion over all the earth. And God saw everything He had made and, behold, it was very good. And the evening and the morning were the sixth day.

(Also see Exodus 20:11)

Creation

Some people try to tell us that the earth fell from the sun.
Others try to tell us that from animals we sprung.
They say it took millions of years for this planet to evolve,
But I can see no problem here that we need try to solve.

Chorus:
For whether it took a million years, or whether it took a day,
To build this world we're living in, here's what I have to say.
The builder is my friend and Lord, I've touched His mighty hand,
And I intend to praise His name, as for His cause I stand.

God told Moses, way back yonder, in the days of old,
And Moses passed it down to us, in Genesis we're told,
How God created earth and man, and all that we behold,
So let us stand for Him, my friend, and fear not, but be bold.

(Repeat Chorus)

That same God who made our world knew just how weak we'd be
He knew that we would sin and then come short of eternity,
So, He prepared a way for us, He sacrificed His Son.
Oh! What a God, He did it all for each and every one.

(Repeat Chorus)

Scripture

Hebrews 4:12-13
For the word of God is quick, and powerful, and sharper than any two edged sword, piercing even to the dividing asunder of soul and spirit, and of the joints and marrow, and is a discerner of the thoughts and intents of the heart. (13) Neither is there any creation that is not manifest in His sight, but all things are naked and opened unto the eyes of Him with whom we have to do.

Psalm 139
O Lord, thou hast searched me, and known me. Thou knowest my downsitting and mine uprising; thou understandeth my thought afar off. Thou compassest my path and my lying down, and art acquainted with all my ways. For there is not a word in my tongue, but, lo O Lord, thou knowest it altogether. Thou hast beset me behind and before, and laid thine hand upon me such knowledge is too wonderful for me; It is high, I cannot attain unto it. Whither shall I go from thy Spirit or whither shall I flee from thy presence? If I ascend up into heaven, thou art there: If I make my bed in hell, behold, thou art there. If I take the wings of the morning, and dwell in the uttermost parts of the sea; even there shall thy hand lead me, and thy right hand shall hold me. If I say, Surely the darkness shall cover me; even the night shall be light about me.
(And continuing through the entire chapter).

Nothing Is Hidden From God

Chorus: (Sing first)

Nothing is hidden from God.
.Nothing is hidden from God.
All our thoughts, all our deeds,
All our wants, all our needs,
Nothing is hidden from God.

Evil thoughts, we may hide them,
Knowing they'll never show.
Evil deeds, done in secret,
No one here may ever know.
We may deceive all our neighbors,
Our family and friends
But...............(Chorus)

We may have a sorrow
We feel we can't share.
We may hide it because
We think no one would care.
But there's one who will comfort,
If only we'll ask
For.................(Chorus)

If you feel something troubling
Your soul from within,
If you've never sought for
Forgiveness from sin,
Don't try to hide how you're feeling
Find peace in the Lord,
For................(Chorus)

Scripture

Revelation 14:6

And I saw another angel fly in the midst of heaven, having the everlasting gospel to preach unto them that dwell on the earth, and to every nation, and kindred, and tongue, and people, saying with a loud voice, Fear God, and give glory to him; for the hour of his judgment is come: and worship him that made heaven, and earth, and the sea, and the fountains of waters.

Revelation 21:1-3

And I saw a new heaven and a new earth: for the first heaven and the first earth were passed away; and there was no more sea. And I John saw the holy city, new Jerusalem, coming down from God out of heaven, prepared as a bride adorned for her husband. And I heard a great voice out of heaven saying, Behold, the tabernacle of God is with men, and he will dwell with them, and shall be with them, and be their God.

Close Encounter

Unidentified flying objects,
People say they're filling the sky.
Causing some to fear and wonder,
If there's life somewhere on high.

Let me tell you this my brother,
We shall see it by and by.
There are angels soaring 'round us,
And a city in the sky.

Chorus:
Do not fear and do not tremble,
All of these wonders you shall see,
If you've had a close encounter
With the Christ of Calvary.

Someday we'll fly without restrictions,
Defy the law of gravity,
Leave a life full of afflictions,
When our soul has been set free.

We'll be identified flying objects,
When we're free of time and space,
For when the King shall call His subjects,
We'll go to join that heavenly race.

(Repeat Chorus)

Scripture

I Peter 5:8-9

Be sober, be vigilant; because your adversary the devil, as a roaring lion, walketh about, seeking whom he may devour: Whom resist steadfast in the faith knowing that the same afflictions are accomplished in your brethren that are in the world.

II Timothy 1:13-14

Hold fast the form of sound words, which thou hast heard of me, in faith and love which is in Christ Jesus. That good thing which was committed unto thee keep by the Holy Ghost which dwelleth in us.

James 4:7-8

Submit yourselves therefore to God. Resist the devil, and he will flee from you.

Get Thee Out Old Satan

Chorus:
*Get thee out, get thee out, get thee out old Satan
Get thee out of the house of the Lord.
Get thee out, get thee out, get thee out old Satan
Get thee out of the house of the Lord!*

*We will sing. We will pray. We will read from the Bible,
We will worship in the house of the Lord.
We can welcome the Spirit, we can pray for the sinner,
When old Satan leaves the house of the Lord, So----
(Repeat Chorus)*

*My body's a house that enfolds God's Spirit,
And it's members are the tools of the Lord.
My voice and my hands are for use in God's service,
So, get out old Satan from this house.
(Repeat Chorus)*

*The Spirit of God will not dwell with the devil.
He won't bless when we're living in sin.
So, let us put out old Satan, let us welcome the Spirit,
And bring joy to the house of the Lord.
(Repeat Chorus)*

Scripture

Philippians 3: 20-21

For our conversation is in heaven; from whence also we look for the Savior, the Lord Jesus Christ: Who shall change our vile body, that it may be fashioned like unto his glorious body, according to the working whereby he is able even to subdue all things unto himself.

I'll Bloom Again

My glass reflects a visage tired and weary.
The lines upon my face have grown with years.
My limbs are tired, my steps are getting slower,
But one day soon, I'll flower once again.

Chorus:
I'll bloom again,
When I reach home in heaven.
I'll bloom again,
Beside a crystal sea,
Green Pastures and my Shepherd
There await me.
Don't weep for me,
Oh no! I'll bloom again.

These tired old eyes will sparkle with new brilliance.
These lips will smile with wonder and with praise.
I'll run through fields abundant and eternal,
When I reach home with God forever more.
(Repeat Chorus)

The lines upon my face don't make me sorrow.
They only tell the trials I've been through.
They tell me that my time is growing nearer,
To meet my Lord and see him face to face.
(Repeat Chorus)

Scripture

Revelation 21:22-23
(Speaking of the holy city, the new Jerusalem)

And I saw no temple therein, for the Lord God Almighty and the Lamb are the temple of it. And the city had no need of the sun, neither of the moon, to shine in it: for the glory of God did lighten it, and the Lamb is the light thereof.

Where The Light Is

Men cling to this world, full of trouble and woe,
On a pathway of darkness they go.
Never seeming to care that the light for their day,
Is only a prayer away.

Chorus:
Where the light is, there is my Savior.
Where the light is, there is my home.
Where the light is, there is forgiveness.
Where the light is, I'm never alone.

"I'm the Light of the World," said my Savior,
And from me all darkness must flee.
If you seek for the light, you can find it,
And from darkness forever be free.
(Repeat Chorus)

There's a city of light called Heaven,
Where no darkness ever can be.
There the Savior will reign forever,
Leave the darkness and come there with me.
(Repeat Chorus)

Scripture

Psalm 23

The Lord is my shepherd;
I shall not want.
He maketh me to lie down in green pastures:
He leadeth me beside the still waters.
He restoreth my soul:
He leadeth me in the paths of righteousness
For His name's sake.
Yea, though I walk through the valley
Of the shadow of death,
I will fear no evil:
For thou art with me;
Thy rod and Thy staff they comfort me.
Thou preparest a table before me
In the presence of mine enemies:
My cup runneth over.
Surely goodness and mercy shall follow me
All the days of my life:
And I will dwell in the house of the Lord for ever.

The Valley of Despair

I was lost in the valley of despair.
I didn't know Christ was also walking there,
Seeking souls that were burdened down with care,
Souls like me in the valley of despair.

I fell upon my knees there in prayer.
I'd lost all hope and thought no one would care.
Then a light shone around me everywhere.
Christ had found me in the valley of despair.

He found me there in the valley of despair.
He lifted me from every burden, every care.
He gave me peace and joy beyond compare.
And freedom from the valley of despair.

Christ lifted me, set my feet on solid ground.
The Son of God lights my pathway all around
Now Joy. Hope, and Peace all abound,
And from the valley of despair, I've been found.

When trials take you to the valley of despair
You need not worry for Christ is also there
He will share every burden, every care,
Just trust in Him through the valley of despair.

Praise God His power and love reached out to me.
When I was blinded by sin and could not see.
He brought faith and love enough to share,
And I no longer fear the valley of despair.

Scripture

St. Luke relates the story of Jesus birth in Chapter two of his book in the Bible. The story of the shepherds' visit begins at verse eight of that chapter. Although these scriptures are the background for the song, the beautiful Christmas story is worthy of reading in its entirety, not only at Christmas, but at any time of the year.

Although not mentioned in the song, the visit of the Wise Men is well known in the Christmas story, but the account of their visit is not recorded in St. Luke. It is related by St. Matthew in Chapter one of his book in the Bible, beginning with verse eighteen.

The Bible Gospels of Matthew, Mark, Luke, and John all look at Christ from a different perspective and, thus their separate accounts are somewhat different:

St. Matthew's perspective was of Jesus as the Messiah, the King of the Jews, and his book reflects that view. [His record of Christ's genealogy is from the royal line of David through Joseph, His adoptive father, showing His right of succession to David's throne.]

St. Mark's perspective was of Jesus, the Servant of mankind. He came to "seek and to save" that which was lost. [There is no genealogy because no one was interested in the genealogy of a servant.]

St. Luke's perspective was of Jesus the man. "God became man and dwelt among us." [The genealogy listed in his book was of the line of David through His human Mother.]

St. John's perspective is related from the spiritual view of Jesus as God our Savior, the one and only perfect sacrifice for our sins. [The genealogy related in John is of the pre-existing and eternal One. He had no beginning and He has no ending.]

One Incredible Moment

*(Inspired by the book "One Incredible Moment"
by Max Lucado)*

*One incredible moment,
The world was changed forever.
On a night in Bethlehem
Jesus Christ was born!*

*One incredible moment,
Shepherds on a hillside,
Watched their flock of sheep that night,
And gazed up at the stars.
When, suddenly, the sky
Was filled with holy angels,
Silver wings glistening bright,
In a heavenly light.
Voices raised, In wondrous praise
And joyous celebration,
Peace on earth, good will to men,
Jesus Christ is born!*

*Shepherds, go to Bethlehem, seek a lowly stable.
There a Virgin maiden, holds a baby boy.
He is the Son of God, Emmanuel, Messiah,
Prince of Peace, King of Kings,
He's the great I AM!*

*One incredible moment,
My life was changed forever,
All because, in Bethlehem,
Jesus Christ was born!*

Scripture

Philippians 4:6-7

      Be careful (anxious) for nothing; but in every thing by prayer and supplication with thanksgiving let your requests be made known unto God. And the peace of God, which passeth all understanding, shall keep your hearts and minds through Christ Jesus.

Ephesians 3:17-19

[This is my wish for everyone who reads this--]
      That Christ may dwell in your hearts by faith; that ye, being rooted and grounded in love, may be able to comprehend with all saints what is the breadth, and length, and depth, and height; and to know the love of Christ, which passeth knowledge, that ye might be filled with all the fullness of God.

Christmas Is Love

Christmas is in the heart of a child,
In the twinkle of a smile,
In the touch of a friendly hand,
Christmas is Love.

Christmas can mean so much to a few,
Just what does it mean to you?
Is it presents and a tree,
Trimmed for everyone to see,
Or is it Love?

Chorus:
Open your heart, let Christ come in,
Receive His peace, find joy within.
Open your heart, this Christmas day,
Let Christ come in and you can say,
Christmas is Love.

Christmas should reflect the Son of God,
His praise ring out with every word,
Tell the story of His birth,
What it meant to all the earth
That Christmas day.
(Repeat Chorus)

About the Author

Ann Ridings is a resident of Huntingdon, Tennessee, and the mother of one son, Mark, who lives in Nashville, TN. She retired from employment with the State of Tennessee in 1999 and returned to Huntingdon to live with her mother. She often said she moved back home so her mother could take care of her. And she did! Opal, her mother, was active, both physically and mentally until just a couple of months before she died at the age of 105 and they enjoyed a wonderful camaraderie during their time together.

For some time now, Ann has worked as secretary for Huntingdon Missionary Baptist Church where she is a member. She is also a member of The HMBC Helping Hands, a group of ladies who provide meals for members of the church who are sick. They also visit with shut-ins and do other charitable works on behalf of the church.

Being a Christian is the most important thing in Ann's life. She experienced salvation when she was twelve years of age and her testimony of that salvation can be read (along with the testimony of others) on the church's website: hmbch.org.

Ann enjoys writing, gardening, cooking, photography, and playing bridge. But, most of all, she loves people! She loves to be with her family, her friends from childhood, her former co-workers, her brothers and sisters at church, and just about everyone she meets. She is looking forward to visiting with all of them in eternity, for there isn't time here to adequately keep in touch.

Second only to God in Ann's life is her son. They are friends as well as mother and son. She credits him for keeping her up to date on the latest computer technologies needed to do her job as secretary and author. She also has him to thank for her love of photography.

At eighty-three, Ann is beginning another phase in her life as an amateur author. Her goal is to enjoy every day the Lord gives her, and to use the days ahead in some meaningful way.

Acknowledgements

I want to thank my son Mark for everything he did to help me get these ramblings into some sort of order and ready for publication.

I also want to thank him for letting me use some of his beautiful photography to illustrate my work. Most of the pictures used were taken in the Great Smoky Mountains National Park or on a cruise through the San Juan Islands, Washington, to Princess Louisa Inlet in British Colombia. The photographs of nature give us a small glimpse of some of God's amazing creations.

All scripture used in this book is from the King James version of the Bible.

Photography

Page 2	Veteran's Memorial at Thomas Park in Huntingdon, TN
Page 17	Cartoon "People" taken at a Fall Festival in Pigeon Forge, TN.
Page 19	Taken in Smoky Mountains National Park near Gatlinburg, TN.
Page 21	Sunrise in the harbor of Coupeville, WA.
Page 23	Taken in Cades Cover near Townsend, TN.
Page 25	Taken in the San Juan Islands, WA.
Page 31	Sunrise in the Smoky Mountains.

Page 37	Ann and Mark 1965
Page 43	Sunset in the Gulf of Mexico
Page 47	In the forest surrounding Princess Louisa Inlet
Page 50	Taken in February of 2010 just before her 100th birthday
Page 55	On vacation in the Smoky Mountains
Page 59	Pirate's Cove Marine Park, British Columbia
Page 61	Taken from my back porch in Huntingdon
Page 63	Roaring Fork Motor Nature Trail near Gatlinburg, TN.
Page 65	Morton Overlook in the Smoky Mountains
Page 67	Roaring Fork Motor Nature Trail near Gatlinburg, TN
Page 69	Taken in the Smokey Mountains
Page 71	Taken at Ober Gatlinburg.
Page 73	Taken in the Great Smoky Mountains (A favorite location for photographers.)